England Church of

The First Prayerbook as Issued by the Authority of the Parliament of the Second Year of King Edward IV

England Church of

The First Prayerbook as Issued by the Authority of the Parliament of the Second Year of King Edward IV

ISBN/EAN: 9783337155018

Printed in Europe, USA, Canada, Australia, Japan

Cover: Foto ©ninafisch / pixelio.de

More available books at **www.hansebooks.com**

THE

FIRST PRAYER-BOOK

AS ISSUED BY

The Authority of the Parliament of the
Second Year of

KING EDWARD VI.

TWELFTH THOUSAND.

James Parker and Co.
6 SOUTHAMPTON-STREET, STRAND, LONDON;
AND BROAD-STREET, OXFORD.
1899.

PRINTED BY JAMES PARKER AND CO., CROWN YARD, OXFORD.

EDITOR'S PREFACE.

ON Jan. 22, 1549[a], the 'Act for Uniformity of Service and Administration of the Sacraments oughout the Realm' was finally returned from e House of Commons, having passed the third ading in the House of Lords on Jan. 15.

The Preamble of this Act states briefly the history of the book. It begins by explaining that much diversity of usage had crept into the Cathedrals and Parish Churches of England and Wales, "as well concerning the Mattens, or Morning Prayer, and the Evensong, as also concerning the Holy Communion, commonly called the Mass, with divers and sundry rites and ceremonies concerning the same, and in the Administration of other Sacraments of the Church."

It then goes on to state that His Highness (K. Edward VI.), "to the intent a uniform, quiet, and godly order should be had concerning the premisses ... hath appointed the Archbishop of Canterbury, and certain of the most learned and

[a] The date is according to the new style, that is, according to our present style of reckoning. In contemporary documents it would be written Jan. 1548, because the year according to the old reckoning did not end until March 25.

discreet Bishops, and other learned men of this realm, to consider and ponder the premisses. And thereupon having as well eye and respect to the most sincere and pure Christian Religion taught by the Scripture, as to the usages in the Primitive Church, should draw and make one convenient order, rite and fashion of common and open prayer, and Administration of the Sacraments, to be had and used in his Majesty's realm of England and in Wales; the which at this time by the aid of the Holy Ghost, with one uniform agreement is of them concluded, set forth and delivered to his highness, to his great comfort and quietness of mind, in a book intituled,—

"'The Book of Common Prayer, and Administration of the Sacraments, and other rites and ceremonies of the Church, after the use of the Church of England.'

"Wherefore the Lords Spiritual and Temporal, and the Commons of this present Parliament assembled ... humbly pray that it may be ordained and enacted by his Majesty ... that all and singular Ministers in any Cathedral or Parish Church ... shall from and after the Feast of Pentecost next coming [June 9, 1549], be bounden to say and use the Mattens, Evensong, Celebration of the Lord's Supper, commonly called the Mass, and administration of each of the Sacraments, and all their common and open Prayer in such order and form as is mentioned in the same book, and none other or otherwise."

The Prayer-Book, then, which had been compiled by the Committee of Bishops and others, was authorized by Parliament. The history of its compilation is somewhat obscure, and though a list of names of compilers is frequently given, there is no good contemporary authority for it. Unfortunately, the Official Records of Convocation for these years were burnt. From a few rough notes accidentally preserved, we find that the Convocation, of which the session had commenced on Nov. 5, 1547, had amongst their Agenda for Nov. 22, "that the works of the Bishops and others, who by the command of the Convocation have laboured in examining, reforming and publishing, the divine Service, may be produced and laid before the examination of this house." During the whole of 1548 we have no records which touch upon their work, but in all probability the same Commission was continued, and it is to this Commission that the Act of Uniformity of Jan., 1549, no doubt refers.

Several editions were at once printed, in order to be ready by the following June, although but small numbers of each; for the process of printing off copies of each sheet was much more tedious than it would be now even with hand-presses; and since the use of steam has so revolutionized the art of printing, it is hard to realize the difficulties then in producing large numbers of copies. Some of the copies of 1549 were no doubt destroyed when the book of 1552 came in, and all that were found of either by the authorities were destroyed when Mary's reign began, though the destruction of the old books would hardly have been so extensive then as when the Puritans had their way some hundred years later, viz. in 1645, and when heavy penalties were enforced upon any found possessing the Book of Common Prayer. It has therefore happened that copies are scarce, and the few which remain belong to different editions. The two chief printers were Whitchurch and Grafton. There are certainly three various editions with the name of Whitchurch, and there are certainly three various editions with that of Grafton, all bearing the date of 1549; but there are difficulties in ascertaining the exact number of editions, for, besides the rarity of copies, some of those which we do find appear to be 'made up,' i.e. sheets of one edition bound up with another. Copies are also found with the imprint of John Oswen of Worcester, and of two distinct printings.

All editions, however, are very similar in substance, the variations being merely a word or so omitted or varied by the printer's carelessness. A glance over the notes of the variations (which are given at the foot of the pages throughout this edition) will shew of what little importance they are. As a rule, the text here given follows an edition of Whitchurch, except when that is evidently erroneous, and the other reading is the right one. In one or two cases, also, when there has been a choice of readings, that which has been adopted in the later editions has been preferred, and the variations put into the note. Of course the copies differ considerably from one another in the use of stops, in the use of capital letters, and in spelling. It may be said that, as regards this class of variations, few lines can be found *exactly* the same in any two copies, if they are of different editions.

The plan here adopted has been to reduce the spelling to the modern way. In the use of stops and of capital letters, the edition before referred to has, as a rule, been followed, excepting when that of another edition has seemed decidedly preferable; only that throughout the names of the Holy Trinity and the like are spelt with capitals. In all original books the name of God is more frequently than not spelt with a small "g," the use of capitals being evidently left entirely to the caprice or convenience of the printer.

As the work is not intended for critical study, it has not been thought necessary to describe what editions, or, indeed, how many editions, had any one particular reading. The fact is, that this could, even with the greatest care, be only given approximately.

It is needless at the present time to speak of the place this little edition is intended to fulfil.

The many attacks on the Prayer-Book, arising often from misunderstanding the character, have called attention to the origin, and the changes which have been made in it from time to time. It has been thought, therefore, that it would be of great advantage to many who would resist such attacks, to have the book, as it came forth from the hands of the English Reformers, readily accessible. It will be seen that several of the controversies of the day arise from uncertain directions given in the later revisions, which in this the first issue are clear and precise.

It is proposed to print and issue, uniform with this, the edition of 1552, namely, the same book after it had been subjected to correction under the influence of the Continental Reformers.

JAMES PARKER.

Turl, Nov. 1882.

THE
BOOK OF THE COMMON PRAYER AND ADMINISTRATION OF THE SACRAMENTS, AND OTHER RITES AND CEREMONIES OF THE CHURCH: AFTER THE USE OF THE CHURCH OF ENGLAND.

Londini in Officina
Edouardi Whitchurche.
Cum privilegio ad imprimendum solum.
Anno Do. 1549, *Mense* Martii.

Various Imprints.

B Same as above, except Anno Do. 1549, Mense Maii
C Ditto, Anno Do. 1549, Mense Junii.
D Londini In Officina Richardi Graftoni Regii Impressoris. *Cum Privilegio ad Imprimendum solum. Anno Domini* M.D.XLIX. Mense Martii.
E Ditto (but a different book).
F Ditto (but a different book).
G H Wigorniæ *in Officina Ioannis* Ofwœni. *cum privilegio ad imprimendum solum.* Anno Do. 1549, Mense Julii.

THE CONTENTS OF THIS BOOK.

i. A Preface.

ii. A Table and Kalendar for Psalms and Lessons, with necessary rules pertaining to the same.

iii. The Order for Matins and Evensong, throughout the year.

iv. The Introits, Collects, Epistles and Gospels, to be used at the celebration of the Lord's Supper and holy Communion through the year, with proper Psalms and Lessons, for divers feasts and days.

v. The Supper of the Lord and holy Communion, commonly called the Mass.

vi. The Litany and Suffrages [b].

vii. Of Baptism, both public and private.

viii. Of Confirmation, where also is a Catechism for children.

ix. Of Matrimony.

x. Of Visitation of the Sick, and Communion of the same.

xi. Of Burial.

xii. The purification of women.

xiii. A declaration of Scripture, with certain prayers to be used the first day of Lent, commonly called Ashwednesday.

xiv. Of Ceremonies omitted or retained.

xv. Certain notes for the more plain explication and decent ministration of things contained in this book.

[b] In one ed., 1549, the Litany is omitted in this place, and given on a supplementary sheet inserted at the end of the book, so that the numbering of the Contents after No. v. is thrown out.

THE PREFACE.

THERE was never any thing by the wit of man so well devised, or so surely established, which (in continuance of time) hath not been corrupted: as (among other things) it may plainly appear by the common prayers in the Church, commonly called divine service: the first original and ground whereof if a man would search out by the ancient fathers, he shall find that the same was not ordained, but of a good purpose, and for a great advancement of godliness: for they so ordered the matter, that all the whole Bible (or the greatest part thereof) should be read over once in the year, intending thereby, that the Clergy, and specially such as were Ministers of the congregation, should (by often reading and meditation of God's word) be stirred up to godliness themselves, and be more able also to exhort other by wholesome doctrine, and to confute them that were adversaries to the truth. And further, that the people (by daily hearing of holy scripture read in the Church) should continually profit more and more in the knowledge of God, and be the more inflamed with the love of his true religion. But these many years passed, this godly and decent order of the ancient fathers hath been so altered, broken, and neglected, by planting in uncertain stories, Legends, Responds, Verses, vain repetitions, Commemorations, and Synodals, that commonly when any book of the Bible was begun, before three or four chapters were read out, all the rest were unread. And in this sort, the book of Esaie was begun in Advent, and the book of Genesis in Septuagesima: but they were only begun, and never read through. After a like sort were other books of holy scripture used. And moreover, whereas St. Paul would have such language spoken to the people in the church, as they might understand and have profit by hearing the same; the service in this Church of England (these many years) hath been read in Latin to the people, which they understood not; so that they have heard with their ears only; and their hearts, spirit, and mind, have not been edified thereby. And furthermore, notwithstanding that the ancient fathers had divided the Psalms into seven portions, whereof every one was called a nocturn; now of late time a few of them have been daily said (and oft repeated) and the rest utterly omitted. Moreover, the number and hardness of the rules called the Pie, and the manifold changings of the service, was the cause, that to turn the book only was so hard and intricate a matter, that many times there was more business to find out what should be read, than to read it when it was found out.

These inconveniences therefore considered, here is set forth such an order, whereby the same shall be redressed. And for a readiness in this matter, here is drawn out a Kalendar for that purpose, which is plain and easy to be understanded; wherein (so much as may be) the reading of holy scripture is so set forth, that all things shall be done in order, without breaking one piece thereof from another. For this cause be cut off Anthems, Responds, Invitatories, and such like things, as did break the continual course of the reading of the scripture. Yet because there is no remedy, but that of necessity there must be some rules: therefore certain rules are here set forth, which as they be few in number, so they be plain and easy to be understanded. So that here you have an order for prayer (as touching the reading of holy scripture) much agreeable to the mind and purpose of the old fathers, and a great deal more profitable and commodious, than that which of late was used. It is more profitable, because here are left out many things, whereof some be untrue, some uncertain, some vain and superstitious: and is ordained nothing to be read, but the very pure word of God, the holy scriptures, or that which is evidently grounded upon the same; and that in such a language and order, as is most easy and plain for the understanding, both of the readers and hearers. It is also more commodious, both for the shortness thereof, and for the plainness of the order, and for that the rules be few and easy. Furthermore, by this order, the curates shall need none other books for their public service, but this book and the Bible: by the means whereof, the people shall not be at so great charge for books, as in time past they have been.

And where heretofore there hath been great diversity in saying and singing in churches within this realm: some following Salisbury use, some Hereford use, some the use of Bangor, some of York, and some of Lincoln: Now from henceforth, all the whole realm shall have but one use. And if any would judge this way more painful, because that all things must be read upon the book, whereas before, by the reason of so often repetition, they could say many things by heart: if those men will weigh their labour, with the profit in knowledge, which daily they shall obtain by reading upon the book, they will not refuse the pain, in consideration of the great profit that shall ensue thereof.

And forsomuch as nothing can, almost, be so plainly set forth, but doubts may rise in the use and practising of the same: to appease all such diversity (if any arise), and for the resolution of all doubts, concerning the manner how to understand, do, and execute the things contained in this book, the parties that so doubt, or diversely take any thing, shall always resort to the Bishop of the Diocese, who by his discretion shall take order for the quieting and appeasing of the same: so that the same order be not contrary to any thing contained in this book.

¶ Though it be appointed in the afore written preface, that all things shall be read and sung in the church, in the English tongue, to the end that the congregation may be thereby edified: yet it is not meant, but when men say Matins and Evensong privately, they may say the same in any language that they themselves do understand. Neither that any man shall be bound to the saying of them, but such as from time to time, in Cathedral and Collegiate Churches, Parish Churches, and Chapels to the same annexed, shall serve the congregation.

THE TABLE AND

KALENDAR, EXPRESSING THE ORDER OF THE PSALMS AND LESSONS, TO BE SAID AT MATINS AND EVENSONG, THROUGHOUT THE YEAR, EXCEPT CERTAIN PROPER FEASTS, AS THE RULES FOLLOWING MORE PLAINLY DECLARE.

THE ORDER HOW THE PSALTER IS APPOINTED TO BE READ.

THE Psalter shall be read through once every month: and because that some months be longer than some other be, it is thought good to make them even by this means.

To every month, as concerning this purpose, shall be appointed just xxx days.

And because January and March hath one day above the said number, and February, which is placed between them both, hath only xxviii days, February shall borrow of either of the months of January and March one day, and so the Psalter which shall be read in February, must be begun the last day of January, and ended the first day of March.

And whereas May, July, August, October and December hath xxxi days apiece, it is ordered that the same Psalms shall be read the last day of the said month[s], which were read the day before: so that the Psalter may be begun again the first day of the next months ensuing.

Now to know what Psalms shall be read every day, look in the Kalendar the number that is appointed for the Psalms, and then find the same number in this Table, and upon that number shall you see, what Psalms shall be said at Matins, and Evensong.

And where the cxix Psalm is divided into xxii portions, and is over long to be read at one time: it is so ordered, that at one time shall not be read above iv or v of the said portions, as you shall perceive to be noted in this Table.

And here is also to be noted, that in this Table, and in all other parts of the service, where any Psalms are appointed, the number is expressed after the great English Bible, which from the ixth Psalm unto the cxlviiith Psalm (following the division of the Ebrues) doth vary in numbers from the common Latin translation.

A TABLE FOR

The Order of the Psalms, to be said at Matins and Evensong.

	Matins.	Evensong.
i.	i, ii, iii, iv, v.	vi, vii, viii.
ii.	ix, x, xi.	xii, xiii, xiv.
iii.	xv, xvi, xvii.	xviii.
iv.	xix, xx, xxi.	xxii, xxiii.
v.	xxiv, xxv, xxvi.	xxvii, xxviii, xxix.
vi.	xxx, xxxi.	xxxii, xxxiii, xxxiv.
vii.	xxxv, xxxvi.	xxxvii.
viii.	xxxviii, xxxix, xl.	xli, xlii, xliii.
ix.	xliv, xlv, xlvi.	xlvii, xlviii, xlix.
x.	l, li, lii.	liii, liv, lv.
xi.	lvi, lvii, lviii.	lix, lx, lxi.
xii.	lxii, lxiii, lxiv.	lxv, lxvi, lxvii.
xiii.	lxviii.	lxix, lxx.
xiv.	lxxi, lxxii.	lxxiii, lxxiv.
xv.	lxxv, lxxvi, lxxvii.	lxxviii.
xvi.	lxxix, lxxx, lxxxi.	lxxxii, lxxxiii, lxxxiv, lxxxv.
xvii.	lxxxvi, lxxxvii, lxxxviii.	lxxxix.
xviii.	xc, xci, xcii.	xciii, xciv.
xix.	xcv, xcvi, xcvii.	xcviii, xcix, c, ci.
xx.	cii, ciii.	civ.
xxi.	cv.	cvi.
xxii.	cvii.	cviii, cix.
xxiii.	cx, cxi, cxii, cxiii.	cxiv, cxv.
xxiv.	cxvi, cxvii, cxviii.	cxix. Inde. iv.
xxv.	Inde. v.	Inde. iv.
xxvi.	Inde. v.	Inde. iv.
xxvii.	cxx, cxxi, cxxii, cxxiii, cxxiv, cxxv.	cxxvi, cxxvii, cxxviii, cxxix, cxxx, cxxxi.
xxviii.	cxxxii, cxxxiii, cxxxiv, cxxxv.	cxxxvi, cxxxvii, cxxxviii.
xxix.	cxxxix, cxl, cxli.	cxlii, cxliii.
xxx.	cxliv, cxlv, cxlvi.	cxlvii, cxlviii, cxlix, cl.

THE ORDER

HOW THE REST OF HOLY SCRIPTURE (BESIDE THE PSALTER) IS APPOINTED TO BE READ.

The Old Testament. The Old Testament is appointed for the first Lessons, at Matins and Evensong, and shall be read through every year once, except certain books and chapters, which be least edifying, and might best be spared, and therefore are left unread.

The New Testament. The New Testament is appointed for the second Lessons, at Matins and Evensong, and shall be read over orderly every year thrice, beside the Epistles and Gospels ; except the Apocalypse, out of the which there be only certain Lessons appointed upon divers proper feasts.

Lessons. And to know what Lessons shall be read every day: find the day of the month in the Kalendar following : and there ye shall perceive the books and chapters, that shall be read for the Lessons, both at Matins and Evensong.

Proper Psalms. And here is to be noted, that whensoever there be any proper Psalms or Lessons appointed for any feast, moveable or unmoveable ; then the Psalms and Lessons appointed in the Kalendar shall be omitted for that time.

Ye must note also, that the Collect, Epistle, and Gospel, appointed for the Sunday, shall serve all the week after, except there fall some feast that hath his proper.

The Leap-year. This is also to be noted, concerning the leap years, that the xxvth day of February, which in leap years is counted for two days, shall in those two days alter neither Psalm nor Lesson : but the same Psalms and Lessons, which be said the first day, shall serve also for the second day.

Also, wheresoever the beginning of any Lesson, Epistle, or Gospel is not expressed, there ye must begin at the beginning of the chapter.

JANUARY.

JANUARY.			*Psalms.*	MATINS.		EVENSONG.	
				1 *Less.*	2 *Less.*	1 *Less.*	2 *Less.*
A	*Kalend.* 1	*Circumci.* 1		Gen. 17	Roma. 2	Deut. 10	Collos. 2
b	4 No. 2		2	Gene. 1	Math. 1	Gene. 2	Roma. 1
c	3 No. 3		3	3	2	4	2
d	Prid. No. 4		4	5	3	6	3
e	*Nonas.* 5		5	7	4	8	4
f	8 Id. 6	*Epiphani.*	6	Esai. 60	Luke 3	Esai. 49	John 2
g	7 Id. 7		7	Gen. 9	Math. 5	Gen. 11	Roma. 5
A	6 Id. 8		8	12	6	13	6
b	5 Id. 9		9	14	7	15	7
c	4 Id. 10		10	16	8	17	8
d	3 Id. 11		11	18	9	19	9
e	Prid. Id. 12		12	20	10	21	10
f	*Idus.* 13		13	22	11	23	11
g	19 kl. 14		14	24	12	25	12
A	18 kl. 15		15	26	13	27	13
b	17 kl. 16		16	28	14	29	14
c	16 kl. 17		17	30	15	31	15
d	15 kl. 18		18	32	16	33	16
e	14 kl. 19		19	34	17	35	1 Cor. 1
f	13 kl. 20		20	36	18	37	2
g	12 kl. 21		21	38	19	39	3
A	11 kl. 22		22	40	20	41	4
b	10 kl. 23		23	42	21	43	5
c	9 kl. 24		24	44	22	45	6
d	8 kl. 25	*Con.Pauli.* 25	25	46	Act. 22	47	Act. 26
e	7 kl. 26		26	48	Mat. 23	49	1 Cor. 7
f	6 kl. 27		27	50	24	Exod. 1	8
g	5 kl. 28		28	Exod. 2	25	3	9
A	4 kl. 29		29	4	26	5	10
b	3 kl. 30		30	6	27	7	11
c	*Prid.* kl. 31		31	8	28	9	12

FEBRUARY.

FEBRUARY.		Psalms.	MATINS.		EVENSONG.	
			1 *Less.*	2 *Less.*	1 *Less.*	2 *Less.*
Kalend.	1	2	Exod. 10	Mark 1	Exod. 11	1 Cor. 13
4 No.	2 *Puri. Ma.*	3	12	2	13	14
3 No.	3	4	14	3	15	15
Prid. No.	4	5	16	4	17	16
Nonas.	5	6	18	5	19	2 Cor. 1
8 Id.	6	7	20	6	21	2
7 Id.	7	8	22	7	23	3
6 Id.	8	9	24	8	32	4
5 Id.	9	10	33	9	34	5
4 Id.	10	11	35	10	40	6
3 Id.	11	12	Leui. 18	11	Leui. 19	7
Prid. Id.	12	13	20	12	Nume. 10	8
Idus.	13	14	Num. 11	13	12	9
16 kl.	14	15	13	14	14	10
15 kl.	15	16	15	15	16	11
14 kl.	16	17	17	16	18	12
13 kl.	17	18	19	Luk. di. 1.	20	13
12 kl.	18	19	21	di. 1	22	Galath. 1
11 kl.	19	20	23	2	24	2
10 kl.	20	21	25	3	26	3
9 kl.	21	22	27	4	28	4
8 kl.	22	23	29	5	30	5
7 kl.	23	24	31	6	32	6
6 kl.	24 *Mathias.*	25	33	7	34	Ephes. 1
5 kl.	25	26	35	8	36	2
4 kl.	26	27	Deut. 1	9	Deut. 2	3
3 kl.	27	28	3	10	4	4
Prid. kl.	28	29	5	11	6	5

MARCH.

	MARCH.		*Psalms.*	MATINS.		EVENSONG.	
				1 *Less.*	2 *Less.*	1 *Less.*	2 *Less.*
d	*Kalend.*	1	30	Deu. 7	Luk. 12	Deu. 8	Ephe. 6
e	6 No.	2	1	9	13	10	Philip. 1
f	5 No.	3	2	11	14	12	2
g	4 No.	4	3	13	15	14	3
A	3 No.	5	4	15	16	16	4
b	Prid. No.	6	5	17	17	18	Collos. 1
c	*Nonas.*	7	6	19	18	20	2
d	8 Id.	8	7	21	19	22	3
e	7 Id.	9	8	23	20	24	4
f	6 Id.	10	9	25	21	26	1 Thes. 1
g	5 Id.	11	10	27	22	28	2
A	4 Id.	12	11	29	23	30	3
b	3 Id.	13	12	31	24	32	4
c	Prid. Id.	14	13	33	John. 1	34	5
d	*Idus.*	15	14	Josue. 1	2	Josue. 2	2 Thes. 1
e	17 kl.	16	15	3	3	4	2
f	16 kl.	17	16	5	4	6	3
g	15 kl.	18	17	7	5	8	1 Timo. 1
A	14 kl.	19	18	9	6	10	2. 3
b	13 kl.	20	19	11	7	12	4
c	12 kl.	21	20	13	8	14	5
d	11 kl.	22	21	15	9	16	6
e	10 kl.	23	22	17	10	18	2 Tim. 1
f	9 kl.	24	23	19	11	20	2
g	8 kl.	25	*Annuncia.* 24	21	12	22	3
A	7 kl.	26	25	23	13	24	4
b	6 kl.	27	26	Judic. 1	14	Judic. 2	Titus 1
c	5 kl.	28	27	3	15	4	2. 3
d	4 kl.	29	28	5	16	6	Phile. 1
e	3 kl.	30	29	7	17	8	Hebre. 1
f	Prid. kl.	31	30	9	18	10	2

APRIL.

	APRIL.		Psalms	MATINS.		EVENSONG.	
				1 Less.	2 Less.	1 Less.	2 Less.
g	Kalend.	1	1	Judi. 11	John 19	Judi. 12	Hebre. 3
A	4 No.	2	2	13	20	14	4
b	3 No.	3	3	15	21	16	5
c	Prid. No.	4	4	17	Acts 1	18	6
d	Nonas.	5	5	19	2	20	7
e	8 Id.	6	6	21	3	Ruth 1	8
f	7 Id.	7	7	Ruth 2	4	3	9
g	6 Id.	8	8	4	5	1Regum1	10
A	5 Id.	9	9	1Regum 2	6	3	11
b	4 Id.	10	10	4	7	5	12
c	3 Id.	11	11	6	8	7	13
d	Prid. Id.	12	12	8	9	9	Jacob. 1
e	Idus.	13	13	10	10	11	2
f	18 kl.	14	14	12	11	13	3
g	17 kl.	15	15	14	12	15	4
A	16 kl.	16	16	16	13	17	5
b	15 kl.	17	17	18	14	19	1 Peter. 1
c	14 kl.	18	18	20	15	21	2
d	13 kl.	19	19	22	16	23	3
e	12 kl.	20	20	24	17	25	4
f	11 kl.	21	21	26	18	27	5
g	10 kl.	22	22	28	19	29	2 Peter. 1
A	9 kl.	23	23	30	20	31	2
b	8 kl.	24	24	2 Reg. 1	21	2 Reg. 2	3
c	7 kl.	25	Mar.Evan 25	3	22	4	1 John. 1
d	6 kl.	26	26	5	23	6	2
e	5 kl.	27	27	7	24	8	3
f	4 kl.	28	28	9	25	10	4
g	3 kl.	29	29	11	26	12	5
A	Prid. kl.	30	30	13	27	14	2. 3. Joh.

MAY.

	MAY.			*Psalms.*	MATINS.		EVENSONG.	
					1 *Less.*	2 *Less.*	1 *Less.*	2 *Less.*
b	*Kalend.*	1	*Phil.&Ja.*	1	2 Re. 15	Acts 8	2 Re. 16	Judas. 1
c	6 No.	2		2	17	28	18	Roma. 1
d	5 No.	3		3	19	Math. 1	20	2
e	4 No.	4		4	21	2	22	3
f	3 No.	5		5	23	3	24	4
g	Prid. No.	6		6	3 Reg. 1	4	3 Reg. 2	5
A	*Nonas.*	7		7	3	5	4	6
b	8 Id.	8		8	5	6	6	7
c	7 Id.	9		9	7	7	8	8
d	6 Id.	10		10	9	8	10	9
e	5 Id.	11		11	11	9	12	10
f	4 Id.	12		12	13	10	14	11
g	3 Id.	13		13	15	11	16	12
A	Prid. Id.	14		14	17	12	18	13
b	*Idus.*	15		15	19	13	20	14
c	17 kl.	16		16	21	14	22	15
d	16 kl.	17		17	4 Reg. 1	15	4 Re. 2	16
e	15 kl.	18		18	3	16	4	1 Cor. 1
f	14 kl.	19		19	5	17	6	2
g	13 kl.	20		20	7	18	8	3
A	12 kl.	21		21	9	19	10	4
b	11 kl.	22		22	11	20	12	5
c	10 kl.	23		23	13	21	14	6
d	9 kl.	24		24	15	22	16	7
e	8 kl.	25		25	17	23	18	8
f	7 kl.	26		26	19	24	20	9
g	6 kl.	27		27	21	25	22	10
A	5 kl.	28		28	23	26	24	11
b	4 kl.	29		29	25	27	1 Esd. 1	12
c	3 kl.	30		30	1 Esd. 2	28	3	13
d	*Prid.* kl.	31		30	4	Mark 1	5	14

JUNE.

	JUNE.		Psalms	MATINS.		EVENSONG.	
				1 *Less.*	2 *Less.*	1 *Less.*	2 *Less.*
e	*Kalend.*	1	1	1 Esd. 6	Mark 2	1 Esd. 7	1 Cor. 15
f	4 No.	2	2	8	3	9	16
g	3 No.	3	3	10	4	2 Esd. 1	2 Cor. 1
A	Prid. No.	4	4	2 Esd. 2	5	3	2
b	*Nonas.*	5	5	4	6	5	3
c	8 Id.	6	6	6	7	7	4
d	7 Id.	7	7	8	8	9	5
e	6 Id.	8	8	10	9	11	6
f	5 Id.	9	9	12	10	13	7
g	4 Id.	10	10	Hester 1	11	Hester 2	8
A	3 Id.	11	*Barna. apo* 11	3	Act. 14	4	Acts 15
b	Prid. Id.	12	12	5	Mar. 12	6	2 Cor. 9
c	*Idus.*	13	13	7	13	8	10
d	18 kl.	14	14	9	14	Job 1	11
e	17 kl.	15	15	Job 2	15	3	12
f	16 kl.	16	16	4	16	5	13
g	15 kl.	17	17	6	Luke 1	7	Gala. 1
A	14 kl.	18	18	8	2	9	2
b	13 kl.	19	19	10	3	11	3
c	12 kl.	20	20	12	4	13	4
d	11 kl.	21	21	14	5	15	5
e	10 kl.	22	22	16	6	17. 18	6
f	9 kl.	23	23	19	7	20	Ephe. 1
g	8 kl.	24	*Na Jo. Ba.* 24	Mala. 3	Mat. 3	Mal. 3	Math. 14
A	7 kl.	25	25	Job 21	Lu. 8	Job 22	Ephe. 2
b	6 kl.	26	26	23	9	24. 25	3
c	5 kl.	27	27	26. 27	10	28	4
d	4 kl.	28	28	29	11	30	5
e	3 kl.	29	*S. Peter.* 29	31	Acts 3	32	Acts 4
f	Prid. kl.	30	30	33	Luke 12	34	Ephe. 6

JULY.

	JULY.		Psalms.	MATINS.		EVENSONG.	
				1 *Less.*	2 *Less.*	1 *Less.*	2 *Less.*
g	*Kalend.*	1	1	Job 35	Luk. 13	Job 36	Philip. 1
A	6 No.	2	2	37	14	38	2
b	5 No.	3	3	39	15	40	3
c	4 No.	4	4	41	16	42	4
d	3 No.	5	5	Prover. 1	17	Prov. 2	Collos. 1
e	Prid. No.	6	6	3	18	4	2
f	*Nonas.*	7	7	5	19	6	3
g	8 Id.	8	8	7	20	8	4
A	7 Id.	9	9	9	21	10	1 Thes. 1
b	6 Id.	10	10	11	22	12	2
c	5 Id.	11	11	13	23	14	3
d	4 Id.	12	12	15	24	16	4
e	3 Id.	13	13	17	John 1	18	5
f	Prid. Id.	14	14	19	2	20	2 Thes. 1
g	*Idus.*	15	15	21	3	22	2
A	17 kl.	16	16	23	4	24	3
b	16 kl.	17	17	25	5	26	1 Timo. 1
c	15 kl.	18	18	27	6	28	2. 3
d	14 kl.	19	19	29	7	30	4
e	13 kl.	20	20	31	8	Eccles. 1	5
f	12 kl.	21	21	Eccles. 2	9	3	6
g	11 kl.	22 *Magdalen.*	22	4	10	5	2 Tim. 1
A	10 kl.	23	23	6	11	7	2
b	9 kl.	24	24	8	12	9	3
c	8 kl.	25 *James Ap.*	25	10	13	11	4
d	7 kl.	26	26	12	14	Jere. 1	Titus. 1
e	6 kl.	27	27	Jere. 2	15	3	2. 3
f	5 kl.	28	28	4	16	5	Phile. 1
g	4 kl.	29	29	6	17	7	Hebre. 1
A	3 kl.	30	30	8	18	9	2
b	Prid. kl.	31	30	10	19	11	3

AUGUST.

AUGUST.			Psalms.	MATINS.		EVENSONG.	
				1 Less.	2 Less.	1 Less.	2 Less.
c	Kalend.	1	1	Jere. 12	John. 20	Jere. 13	Hebr. 4
d	4 No.	2	2	14	21	15	5
e	3 No.	3	3	16	Acts 1	17	6
f	Prid. No.	4	4	18	2	19	7
g	Nonas.	5	5	20	3	21	8
A	8 Id.	6	6	22	4	23	9
b	7 Id.	7	7	24	5	25	10
c	6 Id.	8	8	26	6	27	11
d	5 Id.	9	9	28	7	29	12
e	4 Id.	10	10	30	8	31	13
f	3 Id.	11	11	32	9	33	Jacob. 1
g	Prid. Id.	12	12	34	10	35	2
A	Idus.	13	13	36	11	37	3
b	19 kl.	14	14	38	12	39	4
c	18 kl.	15	15	40	13	41	5
d	17 kl.	16	16	42	14	43	Peter. 1
e	16 kl.	17	17	44	15	45. 46	2
f	15 kl.	18	18	47	16	48	3
g	14 kl.	19	19	49	17	50	4
A	13 kl.	20	20	51	18	52	5
b	12 kl.	21	21	Lament 1	19	Lamen. 2	2 Peter. 1
c	11 kl.	22	22	3	20	4	2
d	10 kl.	23	23	5	21	Ezech. 2	3
e	9 kl.	24 BartApost	24	Ezech. 3	22	6	1 John 1
f	8 kl.	25	25	7	23	13	2
g	7 kl.	26	26	14	24	18	3
A	6 kl.	27	27	33	25	34	4
b	5 kl.	28	28	Dani. 1	26	Dani. 2	5
c	4 kl.	29	29	3	27	4	2. 3 John.
d	3 kl.	30	30	5	28	6	Jude 1
e	Prid. kl.	31	30	7	Math. 1	8	Roma. 1

SEPTEMBER.

SEPTEMBER.		Psalms.	MATINS.		EVENSONG.	
			1 Less.	2 Less.	1 Less.	2 Less.
f Kalend.	1	1	Dani. 9	Math. 2	Dani. 10	Roma. 2
g 4 No.	2	2	11	3	12	3
A 3 No.	3	3	13	4	14	4
b Prid. No.	4	4	Ose. 1	5	Ose. 2. 3	5
c Nonas.	5	5	4	6	5. 6	6
d 8 Id.	6	6	7	7	8	7
e 7 Id.	7	7	9	8	10	8
f 6 Id.	8	8	11	9	12	9
g 5 Id.	9	9	13	10	14	10
A 4 Id.	10	10	Joel 1	11	Joel 2	11
b 3 Id.	11	11	3	12	Amos 1	12
c Prid. Id.	12	12	Amos. 2	13	3	13
d Idus.	13	13	4	14	5	14
e 18 kl.	14	14	6	15	7	15
f 17 kl.	15	15	8	16	9	16
g 16 kl.	16	16	Abdias. 1	17	Jonas. 1	1 Cor. 1
A 15 kl.	17	17	Jon. 2. 3	18	4	2
b 14 kl.	18	18	Miche. 1	19	Miche. 2	3
c 13 kl.	19	19	3	20	4	4
d 12 kl.	20	20	5	21	6	5
e 11 kl.	21 Mathewe.	21	7	22	Naum. 1	6
f 10 kl.	22	22	Naum. 2	23	3	7
g 9 kl.	23	23	Abacuc. 1	24	Abacu. 2	8
A 8 kl.	24	24	3	25	Sopho. 1	9
b 7 kl.	25	25	Soph. 2	26	3	10
c 6 kl.	26	26	Agge. 1	27	Agge. 2	11
d 5 kl.	27	27	Zech. 1	28	Zech. 2. 3	12
e 4 kl.	28	28	4. 5	Marke 1	6	13
f 3 kl.	29 Michael.	29	7	2	8	14
g Prid. kl.	30	30	9	3	10	15

OCTOBER.

OCTOBER.		*Psalms*	MATINS.		EVENSONG.	
			1 *Less.*	2 *Less.*	1 *Less.*	2 *Less.*
A	*Kalend.* 1	1	Zacha. 11	Mark 4	Zacha. 12	1 Cor. 16
b	6 No. 2	2	13	5	14	2 Cor. 1
c	5 No. 3	3	Mala. 1	6	Mala. 2	2
d	4 No. 4	4	3	7	4	3
e	3 No. 5	5	Toby. 1	8	Toby. 2	4
f	Prid. No. 6	6	3	9	4	5
g	*Nonas.* 7	7	5	10	6	6
A	8 Id. 8	8	7	11	8	7
b	7 Id. 9	9	9	12	10	8
c	6 Id. 10	10	11	13	12	9
d	5 Id. 11	11	13	14	14	10
e	4 Id. 12	12	Judith 1	15	Judit. 2	11
f	3 Id. 13	13	3	16	4	12
g	Prid. Id. 14	14	5	Lu. di. 1	6	13
A	*Idus.* 15	15	7	di. 1	8	Gala. 1
b	17 kl. 16	16	9	2	10	2
c	16 kl. 17	17	11	3	12	3
d	15 kl. 18 *Luc. Evan.*	18	13	4	14	4
e	14 kl. 19	19	15	5	16	5
f	13 kl. 20	20	Sap. 1	6	Sapi. 2	6
g	12 kl. 21	21	3	7	4	Ephe. 1
A	11 kl. 22	22	5	8	6	2
b	10 kl. 23	23	7	9	8	3
c	9 kl. 24	24	9	10	10	4
d	8 kl. 25	25	11	11	12	5
e	7 kl. 26	26	13	12	14	6
f	6 kl. 27	27	15	13	16	Philip. 1
g	5 kl. 28 *Sy. & Ju.*	28	17	14	18	2
A	4 kl. 29	29	19	15	Eccls. 1	3
b	3 kl. 30	30	Eccls. 2	16	3	4
c	*Prid.* kl. 31	30	4	17	5	Collos. 1

NOVEMBER.

NOVEMBER.			Psalms.		MATINS.		EVENSONG.	
					1 Less.	2 Less.	1 Less.	2 Less.
d	Kalend.	1 AllSaints.	1		Sap. 3	He.11.12	Sap. 5	Apoc. 19
e	4 No.	2	2		Eccle. 6	Lu. 18	Eccle. 7	Collos. 2
f	3 No.	3	3		8	19	9	3
g	Prid.	4	4		10	20	11	4
A	Nonas.	5	5		12	21	13	1 Thes. 1
b	8 Id.	6	6		14	22	15	2
c	7 Id.	7	7		16	23	17	3
d	6 Id.	8	8		18	24	19	4
e	5 Id.	9	9		20	John 1	21	5
f	4 Id.	10	10		22	2	23	2 Thes. 1
g	3 Id.	11	11		24	3	25	2
A	Prid. Id.	12	12		26	4	27	3
b	Idus.	13	13		28	5	29	1 Timo. 1
c	18 kl.	14	14		30	6	31	2. 3
d	17 kl.	15	15		32	7	33	4
e	16 kl.	16	16		34	8	35	5
f	15 kl.	17	17		36	9	37	6
g	14 kl.	18	18		38	10	39	2 Tim. 1
A	13 kl.	19	19		40	11	41	2
b	12 kl.	20	20		42	12	43	3
c	11 kl.	21	21		44	13	45	4
d	10 kl.	22	22		46	14	47	Titus 1
e	9 kl.	23	23		48	15	49	2. 3
f	8 kl.	24	24		50	16	51	Phile. 1
g	7 kl.	25	25		Baruc. 1	17	Baruc. 2	Hebre. 1
A	6 kl.	26	26		3	18	4	2
b	5 kl.	27	27		5	19	6	3
c	4 kl.	28	28		Esay. 1	20	Esay. 2	4
d	3 kl.	29	29		3	21	4	5
e	Prid. kl.	30 AndreApo	30		5	Acts 1	6	6

DECEMBER.

	DECEMBER.		Psalms	MATINS.		EVENSONG.	
				1 *Less.*	2 *Less.*	1 *Less.*	2 *Less.*
f	*Kalend.*	1	1	Esai. 7	Actes 2	Esai. 8	Hebr. 7
g	4 No.	2	2	9	3	10	8
A	3 No.	3	3	11	4	12	9
b	Prid. No.	4	4	13	5	14	10
c	*Nonas.*	5	5	15	6	16	11
d	8 Id.	6	6	17	di. 7	18	12
e	7 Id.	7	7	19	di. 7	20. 21	13
f	6 Id.	8	8	22	8	23	Jacob. 1
g	5 Id.	9	9	24	9	25	2
A	4 Id.	10	10	26	10	27	3
b	3 Id.	11	11	28	11	29	4
c	Prid. Id.	12	12	30	12	31	5
d	*Idus.*	13	13	32	13	33	1 Peter. 1
e	19 kl.	14	14	34	14	35	2
f	18 kl.	15	15	36	15	37	3
g	17 kl.	16	16	38	16	39	4
A	16 kl.	17	17	40	17	41	5
b	15 kl.	18	18	42	18	43	2 Peter. 1
c	14 kl.	19	19	44	19	45	2
d	13 kl.	20	20	46	20	47	3
e	12 kl.	21 *Tho. Apost*	21	48	21	49	1 John. 1
f	11 kl.	22	22	50	22	51	2
g	10 kl.	23	23	52	23	53	3
A	9 kl.	24 [*mini.*	24	54	24	55	4
b	8 kl.	25 *Nati. Do-*	25	Esay. 9	Math. 1	Esay. 7	Tit. 3
c	7 kl.	26 *Stephan.*	26	56	Act. 6. 7	57	Actes 7
d	6 kl.	27 *JohnEvan.*	27	58	Apoc. 1	59	Apo. 22
e	5 kl.	28 *Innocen.*	28	Jer. 31	Acte 25	60	1 John 5
f	4 kl.	29	29	Esay. 61	26	62	2 John 1
g	3 kl.	30	30	63	27	64	3 John 1
A	Prid. kl.	31	30	65	28	66	Jude 1

[*See for Ornaments Rubrick p.* 171.]

AN ORDER

FOR MATINS, DAILY THROUGH THE YEAR.

The Priest being in the quire, shall begin with a loud voice the Lord's Prayer, called the Pater noster.

OUR Father, which art in heaven, hallowed be thy name. Thy kingdom come. Thy will be done in earth as it is in heaven. Give us this day our daily bread. And forgive us our trespasses, as we forgive them that trespass against us. And lead us not into temptation. But deliver us from evil. Amen.

Then likewise he shall say,

O Lord, open thou my lips.

Answer.

And my mouth shall shew forth thy praise.

Priest.

O God, make speed* to save me.

Answer.

O Lord, make haste to help me.

Priest.

Glory be to the Father, and to the Son, and to the Holy Ghost.

As it was in the beginning, is now, and ever shall be world without end. Amen.

Praise ye the Lord.

And from Easter to Trinity Sunday,

Alleluia.

Then shall be said or sung without any Invitatory this Psalm. Venite, exultemus, *&c. in English, as followeth:*

Psalm xcv.

O COME let us sing unto the Lord : let us heartily rejoice in the strength of our salvation.

---

* In some copies, "good speed."

Let us come before his presence with thanksgiving : and shew ourself glad in him with Psalms.

For the Lord is a great God : and a great King, above all gods :

In his hand are all the corners of the earth : and the strength of the hills is his also.

The sea is his, and he made it : and, his hands prepared the dry land.

O come, let us worship and fall down : and kneel before the Lord our Maker.

For he is (the Lord) our God : and we are the people of his pasture, and the sheep of his hands.

To day if ye will hear his voice, harden not your hearts : as in the provocation, and as in the day of temptation in the wilderness.

When your fathers tempted me : proved me, and saw my works.

Forty year long was I grieved with this generation, and said : it is a people that do err in their hearts, for they have not known my ways.

Unto whom I sware in my wrath : that they should not enter into my rest.

Glory be to the Father, and to the Son : and to the Holy Ghost. As it was in the beginning, is now, and ever shall be : world without end. Amen.

Then shall follow certain Psalms in order as they been appointed in a table made for that purpose, except there be proper Psalms appointed for that day. And at the end of every Psalm throughout the year, and likewise in the end of Benedictus, Benedicite, Magnificat, *and* Nunc Dimittis, *shall be repeated.*

Glory be to the Father, and to the Son, &c.

Then shall be read two lessons distinctly with a loud voice, that the people may hear. The first of the Old Testament, the second of the New; like as they be appointed by the Kalendar, except there be proper lessons assigned for that day: the minister that readeth the lesson, standing

MATINS.

and turning him so as he may best be heard of all such as be present. And before every lesson, the minister shall say thus. The first, second, third or fourth chapter of Genesis *or* Exodus, Matthew, Mark, *or other like as is appointed in the Kalendar. And in the end of every Chapter, he shall say.*

¶ Here endeth such a chapter of such a book.

And (to the end the people may the better hear) in such places where they do sing, there shall the lessons be sung in a plain tune after the manner of distinct reading: and likewise the Epistle and Gospel.

After the first lesson shall follow Te Deum laudamus, *in English, daily throughout the year, except in Lent, all the which time in the place of* Te Deum *shall be used* Benedicite omnia Opera Domini Domino, *in English as followeth:*

Te Deum Laudamus [b].

We praise thee, O God, we knowledge thee to be the Lord.

All the earth doth worship thee, the Father everlasting.

To thee all Angels cry aloud, the heavens and all the powers therein.

To thee Cherubin, and Seraphin continually do cry, Holy, holy, holy, Lord God of Sabaoth.

Heaven and earth are replenished with the majesty of thy glory.

The glorious company of the Apostles, praise thee.

The goodly fellowship of the Prophets, praise thee.

The noble army of Martyrs, praise thee.

The holy church throughout all the world doth knowledge thee.

The Father of an infinite majesty.

Thy honourable, true, and only Son.

Also the Holy Ghost [c] the Comforter.

---

[b] In some copies the title runs, "The Praise of God the Father; the Son; and the Holy Ghost."

[c] In some copies, "The Holy Ghost also being the Comforter."

Thou art the King of Glory, O Christ.

Thou art the everlasting Son of the Father.

When thou tookest upon thee to deliver man, thou didst not abhor the virgin's womb.

When thou hadst overcomed the sharpness of death, thou didst open the kingdom of heaven to all believers.

Thou sittest on the right hand of God, in the Glory of the Father.

We believe that thou shalt come to be our judge.

We therefore pray thee, help thy servants, whom thou hast redeemed with thy precious blood.

Make them to be numbered with thy saints, in glory everlasting.

O Lord, save thy people : and bless thine heritage.

Govern them, and lift them up for ever.

Day by day we magnify thee.

And we worship thy name ever world without end.

Vouchsafe, O Lord, to keep us this day without sin.

O Lord, have mercy upon us : have mercy upon us.

O Lord, let thy mercy lighten upon us : as our trust is in thee.

O Lord, in thee have I trusted : let me never be confounded.

Benedicite omnia opera Domini Domino.

O ALL ye works of the Lord, speak good of the Lord : praise him, and set him up for ever.

O ye Angels of the Lord, speak good of the Lord : praise him, and set him up for ever.

O ye heavens, speak good of the Lord : praise him, and set him up for ever.

O ye waters that be above the firmament, speak good of the Lord : praise him, and set him up for ever.

O all ye powers of the Lord, speak good of the Lord : praise him, and set him up for ever.

O ye Sun, and Moon, speak good of the Lord : praise him, and set him up for ever.

O ye stars of heaven, speak good of the Lord : praise him, and set him up for ever.

O ye showers, and dew, speak good of the Lord : praise him, and set him up for ever.

O ye winds of God, speak good of the Lord : praise him, and set him up for ever.

O ye fire and heat, praise ye the Lord : praise him, and set him up for ever.

O ye winter and summer, speak good of the Lord : praise him, and set him up for ever.

O ye dews and frosts, speak good of the Lord : praise him, and set him up for ever.

O ye frost and cold, speak good of the Lord : praise him, and set him up for ever.

O ye ice and snow, speak good of the Lord : praise him, and set him up for ever.

O ye nights and days, speak good of the Lord : praise him, and set him up for ever.

O ye light and darkness, speak good of the Lord : praise him, and set him up for ever.

O ye lightnings and clouds, speak good of the Lord : praise him, and set him up for ever.

O let the earth speak good of the Lord : yea, let it praise him, and set him up for ever.

O ye mountains and hills, speak good of the Lord : praise him, and set him up for ever.

O all ye green things upon the earth, speak good of the Lord : praise him, and set him up for ever.

O ye wells, speak good of the Lord : praise him, and set him up for ever.

O ye seas, and floods, speak good of the Lord : praise him, and set him up for ever.

O ye whales, and all that move in the waters, speak good of the Lord : praise him, and set him up for ever.

O all ye fowls of the air, speak good of the Lord : praise him, and set him up for ever.

O all ye beasts, and cattle, speak ye good of the Lord : praise him, and set him up for ever.

O ye children of men, speak good of the Lord : praise him, and set him up for ever.

O let Israel speak good of the Lord : praise him, and set him up for ever.

O ye priests of the Lord, speak good of the Lord : praise him, and set him up for ever.

O ye servants of the Lord, speak good of the Lord : praise him, and set him up for ever.

O ye spirits and souls of the righteous, speak good of the Lord : praise him, and set him up for ever.

O ye holy and humble men of heart, speak ye good of the Lord : praise ye him, and set him up for ever.

O Ananias, Azarias, and Misael, speak ye good of the Lord : praise ye him, and set him up for ever.

Glory be to the Father, and to the Son : and to the Holy Ghost.

As it was in the beginning, is now, &c.

And after the Second Lesson, throughout the whole year, shall be used Benedictus Dominus Deus Israel, *&c. in English, as followeth :*

Benedictus[d]. Luc. i.

BLESSED be the Lord God of Israel : for he hath visited and redeemed his people;

And hath lifted up an horn of salvation to us : in the house of his servant David;

As he spake by the mouth of his holy Prophets : which hath been since the world began;

That we should be saved from our enemies : and from the hands of all that hate us;

To perform the mercy promised to our fathers : and to remember his holy covenant;

To perform the oath which he sware to our father Abraham : that he would give us;

That we being delivered out of the hands of our enemies : might serve him without fear;

---

[d] In some copies the title runs, "The Song of Zachary ; *Benedictus*: and Thanksgiving for the performance of God's promises."

In holiness and righteousness before him : all the days of our life.

And thou, Child, shalt be called the Prophet of the Highest : for thou shalt go before the face of the Lord, to prepare his ways ;

To give knowledge of salvation unto his people : for the remission of their sins,

Through the tender mercy of our God : whereby the day-spring from on high hath visited us ;

To give light to them that sit in darkness, and in the shadow of death : and to guide our feet into the way of peace.

Glory be to the Father, and to the Son, &c.

As it was in the beginning, is now, and ever, &c.

Then shall be said daily through the year, the prayers following, as well at Evensong as at Matins, all devoutly kneeling.

Lord, have mercy upon us. Christ, have mercy upon us.

Lord, have mercy upon us.

Then the Minister shall say the Creed *and the Lord's Prayer in English, with a loud voice, &c.*

Answer. But deliver us from evil. Amen.

Priest. O Lord, shew thy mercy upon us.

Answer. And grant us thy salvation.

Priest. O Lord, save the king.

Answer. And mercifully hear us when we call upon thee.

Priest. Endue thy ministers with righteousness.

Answer. And make thy chosen people joyful.

Priest. O Lord, save thy people.

Answer. And bless thine inheritance.

Priest. Give peace in our time, O Lord.

Answer. Because there is none other that fighteth for us, but only thou, O God.

Priest. O God, make clean our hearts within us.

Answer. And take not thine holy Spirit from us.

Priest. The Lord be with you.
Answer. And with thy spirit.

Then shall daily follow three Collects. The first of the day, which shall be the same that is appointed at the Communion. The second for peace. The third for grace to live well. And the two last Collects shall never alter, but daily be said at Matins throughout all the year, as followeth: the Priest standing up, and saying,

Let us pray.

¶ *Then the Collect of the day.*
¶ *The second Collect: for peace.*

O GOD, which art author of peace, and lover of concord, in knowledge of whom standeth our eternal life, whose service is perfect freedom: defend us, thy humble servants, in all assaults of our enemies, that we, surely trusting in thy defence, may not fear the power of any adversaries: through the might of Jesu Christ our Lord. Amen.

The third Collect: for grace.

O LORD, our heavenly Father, almighty and everliving God, which hast safely brought us to the beginning of this day: defend us in the same with thy mighty power; and grant that this day we fall into no sin, neither run into any kind of danger, but that all our doings may be ordered by thy governance, to do always that is righteous in thy sight: through Jesus Christ our Lord. Amen.

AN ORDER
FOR EVENSONG
THROUGHOUT THE YEAR.

The Priest shall say.

OUR Father, &c.

Then likewise he shall say.

O God, make speed to save me.

Answer.

O Lord, make haste to help me.

Priest.

Glory be to the Father, and to the Son : and to the Holy Ghost;

As it was in the beginning, is now, and ever shall be : world without end.   Amen.

Praise ye the Lord.

And from Easter to Trinity Sunday.

Alleluia.

As before is appointed at Matins.

Then Psalms in order as they be appointed in the Table for Psalms, except there be proper Psalms appointed for that day. Then a Lesson of the Old Testament, as it is appointed likewise in the Calendar, except there be proper Lessons appointed for that day. After that, (Magnificat anima mea Dominum) *in English, as followeth.*

Magnificat[*].   Luc. i.

MY soul doth magnify the Lord.

And my spirit hath rejoiced in God my Saviour.

For he hath regarded the lowliness of his handmaiden.

---

[*] In some copies, "The Song of Mary rejoicing and praising God," *instead of* "Magnificat," *and printed on a separate sheet at the close of the volume.*

For behold, from henceforth all generations shall call me blessed.

For he that is mighty hath magnified me : and holy is his name.

And his mercy is on them that fear him : throughout all generations.

He hath shewed strength with his arm : he hath scattered the proud in the imagination of their hearts.

He hath put down the mighty from their seat : and hath exalted the humble and meek.

He hath filled the hungry with good things : and the rich he hath sent empty away.

He remembering his mercy, hath holpen his servant Israel : as he promised to our fathers, Abraham and his seed, for ever.

Glory be to the Father, and to the Son, &c.

As it was in the beginning, &c.

Then a Lesson of the New Testament. And after that (Nunc dimittis servum tuum) *in English as followeth.*

Nunc Dimittis[f]. Luc. ii.

LORD, now lettest thou thy servant depart in peace : according to thy word.

For mine eyes have seen : thy salvation.

Which thou hast prepared : before the face of all[g] people ;

To be a light[h] to lighten the Gentiles : and to be the glory of thy people[i] Israel.

Glory be to the Father, and to the Son : and to the Holy Ghost.

As it was in the beginning, is now, and ever shall be : world without end. Amen.

---

[f] In some copies, "The Song of Symeon the Just," *instead of* "Nunc dimittis," *and printed on a separate sheet.*

[g] In some copies, "all thy;" and in other, "of thy."

[h] In some copies, "for to lighten."   [i] In some copies, "of Israel."

Then the suffrages before assigned at Matins, the clerks kneeling likewise, with three Collects. First of the day: Second of peace: Third for aid against all perils, as here followeth. Which two last Collects shall be daily said at Evensong without alteration.

The second Collect at Evensong.

O GOD, from whom all holy desires, all good counsels, and all just works do proceed: Give unto thy servants that peace. which the world cannot give; that both our hearts may be set to obey thy commandments, and also that by thee we being defended from the fear of our enemies, may pass our time in rest and quietness: through the merits of Jesu Christ our Saviour. Amen.

The third Collect for aid against all perils.

LIGHTEN our darkness, we beseech thee, O Lord. and by thy great mercy, defend us from all perils and dangers of this night, for the love of thy only Son, our Saviour Jesu Christ. Amen.

¶ *In the feasts of* Christmas, the Epiphany, Easter, the Ascension, Pentecost, *and upon* Trinity *Sunday, shall be sung or said immediately after* Benedictus *this Confession of our Christian Faith.*

Quicunque vult, &c.

WHOSOEVER will be saved: before all things it is necessary that he hold the Catholic faith.

Which faith except every one do keep holy and undefiled: without doubt he shall perish everlastingly.

And the Catholic faith is this: That we worship one God in Trinity, and Trinity in Unity;

Neither confounding the persons: nor dividing the substance.

For there is one person of the Father, another of the Son: and another of the Holy Ghost.

But the Godhead of the Father, of the Son, and of the Holy Ghost, is all one : the glory equal, the majesty co-eternal.

Such as the Father is, such is the Son : and such is the Holy Ghost.

The Father uncreate, the Son uncreate : and the Holy Ghost uncreate.

The Father incomprehensible, the Son incomprehensible : and the Holy Ghost incomprehensible.

The Father eternal, the Son eternal : and the Holy Ghost eternal.

And yet they are not three eternals : but one eternal.

As also there be not three incomprehensibles, nor three uncreated : but one uncreated, and one incomprehensible.

So likewise the Father is almighty, the Son almighty : and the Holy Ghost Almighty.

And yet are they not three almighties : but one almighty.

So the Father is God, the Son God : and the Holy Ghost God.

And yet are they not three God : but one God.

So likewise the Father is Lord, the Son Lord : and the Holy Ghost Lord.

And yet not three Lords : but one Lord.

For like as we be compelled by the Christian verity[k] : to acknowledge every person by himself to be God and Lord :

So are we forbidden by the Catholic religion : to say there be three Gods, or three Lords.

The Father is made of none : neither created nor begotten.

The Son is of the Father alone : not made nor created, but begotten.

The Holy Ghost is of the Father and of the Son :

---

[k] In some copies, " Christian unity "

neither made nor created, nor begotten, but proceeding.

So there is one Father, not three Fathers; one Son, not three Sons : one Holy Ghost, not three Holy Ghosts.

And in this Trinity none is afore nor[1] after other : none is greater nor less than other.

But the whole three persons : be co-eternal together and co-equal.

So that in all things, as is[m] aforesaid : the Unity in Trinity, and the Trinity in Unity is to be worshipped.

He therefore that will be saved : must thus think of the Trinity.

Furthermore, it is necessary to everlasting salvation : that he also believe rightly in the Incarnation of our Lord Jesu Christ.

For the right faith is that we believe and confess : that our Lord Jesus Christ, the Son of God, is God and man ;

God of the Substance of the Father, begotten before the worlds : and man of the substance of his mother, born in the world.

Perfect God, and perfect man : of a reasonable soul, and human flesh subsisting.

Equal to the Father as touching his Godhead : and inferior to the Father[n] touching his manhood.

Who although he be God and man : yet he is not two, but one Christ.

One, not by conversion of the Godhead into flesh : but by taking of the manhood into God ;

One altogether, not by confusion of substance : **but by unity of person.**

For as the reasonable soul and flesh is one **man** : so God and man is one Christ.

---

[1] In some copies, "or."   [m] In some copies, "as it is."
[n] In some copies, "as touching."

Who suffered for our salvation : descended into hell, rose again the third day from the dead.

He ascended into heaven, he sitteth on the right hand of the Father, God Almighty : from whence he shall come to judge the quick and dead.

At whose coming all men shall rise again with their bodies : and shall give account of their own works.

And they that have done good, shall go into life everlasting : and they that have done evil, into everlasting fire.

This is the Catholic faith : which except a man believe faithfully, he cannot be saved.

Glory be to the Father, and to the Son : and to the Holy Ghost.

As it was in the beginning, is now, and ever shall be : world without end. Amen.

Thus endeth the Order of Matins and Evensong through the whole Year.

THE INTROITS[r],

COLLECTS, EPISTLES, AND GOSPELS, TO BE USED AT THE CELEBRATION OF THE LORD'S SUPPER AND HOLY COMMUNION, THROUGH THE YEAR:
WITH PROPER PSALMS AND LESSONS FOR DIVERS FEASTS AND DAYS.

¶ *The first Sunday in Advent.*
Beatus vir. Psalm i.

BLESSED is that man that hath not walked ... [&c.]
Glory be to the Father, and to the Son, and to the Holy Ghost;
As it was in the beginning, and is now, and ever shall be : world without end. Amen.

And so must every Introit be ended.

Let us pray.

The Collect.

ALMIGHTY God, give us grace that we may cast away the works of darkness, and put upon us the armour of light, now in the time of this mortal life, (in the which thy Son Jesus Christ came to visit us in great humility:) that in the last day, when he shall come again in his glorious majesty, to judge both the quick and the dead, we may rise to the life immortal, through him, who liveth and reigneth with thee and the Holy Ghost, now and ever. Amen.

The Epistle. Rom. xiii. Owe nothing to any man but this ..... [&c.]
[i.e. Rom. xiii. verse 8 to the end.]

The Gospel. Matt. xxi. And when they drew nigh, to Jerusalem ..... [&c.]
[i.e. Matt. xxi. verse 1 to the end.]

---

[r] The Introits, Epistles and Gospels are printed entire in all the copies of the Prayer-Book, but it has not been thought necessary to print them so in the following pages. It should be mentioned that the reference to the portion appointed is exclusive of the last verse named, i.e. to verse 14 means to end of verse 13.

The second Sunday.

Ad Dominum cum tribularer.   Psalm cxx.

WHEN I was in trouble I called upon the Lord, [&c.]

The Collect.

BLESSED Lord, which hast caused all holy scriptures to be written for our learning : grant us that we may in such wise hear them, read, mark, learn, and inwardly digest them, that by patience and comfort of thy holy word, we may embrace and ever hold fast the blessed hope of everlasting life, which thou hast given us in our Saviour Jesus Christ.

The Epistle.   Roma. xv.   Whatsoever things are written . . . . .   [&c.]
[i.e. Rom. xv. verse 4 to verse 14.]

The Gospel.   Luc. xxi.   There shall be signs in the sun and in the moon . . . . .   [&c.]
[i.e. Luke xxi. verse 25 to verse 34.]

The third Sunday.

Cum invocarem.   Psalm iv.

HEAR me when I call, O God . . . . .   [&c.]

The Collect.

LORD, we beseech thee, give ear to our prayers, and by thy gracious visitation lighten the darkness of our heart, by our Lord Jesus Christ.

The Epistle.   1 Cori. iv.   Let a man this wise esteem . . . . .   [&c.]
[i.e. 1 Cor. iv. verse 1 to verse 6.]

The Gospel.   Math. xi.   When John being in prison heard the works . . . . .   [&c.]
[i.e. Mat. xi. verse 2 to verse 11.]

¶ The fourth Sunday.

Verba mea auribus.   Psalm v.

PONDER my words, O Lord : consider . . . . . [&c.]

AT THE COMMUNION.

The Collect.

LORD, raise up (we pray thee) thy power, and come among us, and with great might succour us, that whereas through our sins and wickedness we be sore let and hindered, thy bountiful grace and mercy, through the satisfaction of thy Son our Lord, may speedily deliver us; to whom with thee and the Holy Ghost be honour and glory world without end.

The Epistle. Philip. iv. Rejoice in the Lord alway, and again . . . . . [&c.]
[i.e. Phil. iv. verse 4 to verse 8.]

The Gospel. John i. This is the record of John, when the Jews . . . . . [&c.]
[i.e. John i. verse 19 to verse 29.]

Proper Psalms and Lessons on Christmas Day.

¶ *At Matins.*

Psalms xix. xlv. lxxxv.

The first lesson, Esai. ix. *unto the end.*
The second lesson, Math. i. *unto the end.*

¶ *At the first Communion.*

Cantate Domino. Psalm xcviii.

O SING unto the Lord a new song: for he . . . [&c.]

The Collect.

GOD, which makest us glad with the yearly remembrance of the birth of thy only Son Jesus Christ: grant that as we joyfully receive him for our Redeemer, so we may with sure confidence behold him, when he shall come to be our Judge, who liveth and reigneth, &c.

The Epistle. Tit. ii. The grace of God that bringeth . . . . . [&c.]
[i.e. Tit. ii. verse 11 to the end.]

The Gospel. Luc. ii. And it chanced in those days that there went . . . . . [&c.]
[i.e. Luke ii. to verse 15.]

¶ *At the second Communion.*

Domine Dominus noster.   Psalm viii.

O LORD our governour, how excellent ..... [&c.]

The Collect.

ALMIGHTY God, which hast given us thy only-begotten Son to take our nature upon him, and this day to be born of a pure virgin; Grant that we being regenerate, and made thy children by adoption and grace, may daily be renewed by thy holy Spirit, through the same our Lord Jesus Christ, who liveth and reigneth, &c.

The Epistle. Hebre. i. God in times past diversely ..... [&c.]

[i.e. Heb. i. verse 1 to verse 13.]

The Gospel. John i. In the beginning was the Word ..... [&c.]

[i.e. John i. verse 1 to verse 15.]

Proper Psalms and lessons at Evensong.   Psalms lxxxix. cx. cxxxii.

The first lesson, Esai. vii. "God spake once again to Achas," &c. . . *unto the end.*

The second lesson, Tit. iii. "The kindness and love of our Saviour," &c. *unto* "foolish questions."

¶ *Saint Stephin's Day.*

¶ *At Matins.*

The second lesson, Acts vi. vii. "Stephin full of faith and power," *unto,* "And when forty years."

At the Communion.   Quid gloriaris in malicia?   Psalm lii.

Why boastest thou thyself, thou tyrant ..... [&c.]

The Collect.

GRANT us, O Lord, to learn to love our enemies by the example of thy martyr Saint Stephen, who prayed to thee for his persecutors : which livest and reignest, &c.

Then shall follow a collect of the Nativity.

The Epistle. Acts vii. And Stephen being full of the Holy Ghost . . . . . [&c.]
[i.e. Acts vii. verse 55 to the end.]

The Gospel. Math. xxiii. Behold, I send unto you prophets and wise men . . . . . [&c.]
[i.e. Matt. xxiii. verse 34 to the end.]

The second Lesson at Evensong.

Acts vii. ¶ "And when forty years were expired, there appeared unto Moses," *unto* "Stephin full of the Holy Ghost," &c.

¶ *Saint John Evangelist's Day.*

At Matins.

¶ The second lesson, Apoca. i. *unto the end.*

At the Communion.

In Domino confido. Psalm xi.

IN the Lord put I my trust : how . . . . . [&c.]

The Collect.

MERCIFUL Lord, we beseech thee to cast thy bright beams of light upon thy Church : that it being lightened by the doctrine of thy blessed Apostle and Evangelist John may attain to thy everlasting gifts : through Jesus Christ our Lord.

The Epistle. 1 John i. That which was from the beginning . . . . . [&c.]
[i.e. 1 John i. verse 1 to the end.]

The Gospel. John xxi. Jesus said unto Peter . . [&c.]
[i.e. John xxi. verse 19 to the end.]

¶ *At Evensong.*

¶ The second lesson, Apoca. xxii. *unto the end.*

¶ *The Innocents' Day.*
¶ *At Matins.*

¶ The first lesson, Hiere. xxxi. *unto,* "Moreover I heard Ephraim."

Deus, venerunt gentes. Psalm lxxix.

O GOD, the heathen are come into thine inheritance..... [&c.]

The Collect.

ALMIGHTY God, whose praise this day the young innocents thy witnesses hath confessed, and shewed forth, not in speaking, but in dying: mortify and kill all vices in us, that in our conversation, our life may express thy faith, which with our tongues we do confess: through Jesus Christ our Lord.

The Epistle. Apoca. xiv. I looked, and lo a lamb stood on the..... [&c.]
[i.e. Apoc. xiv. verse 1 to verse 6.]

The Gospel. Math. ii. The angel of the Lord appeared..... [&c.]
[i.e. Matt. ii. verse 13 to verse 19.]

¶ *The Sunday after Christmas Day.*

Levavi oculos. Psalm cxxi.

I WILL lift up mine eyes unto the hills..... [&c.]

The Collect.

ALMIGHTY God, which hast given us, &c., *as upon Christmas Day.*

The Epistle. Gala. iv. And I say, that the heir as long as..... [&c.]
[i.e. Gal. iv. verse 1 to verse 8.]

The Gospel. Math. i. This is the book of the generation..... [&c.]
[i.e. Matt. i. verse 1 to the end.]

¶ *The Circumcision of Christ.*
At Matins.

The first lesson, Gene. xvii. *unto the end.*
The second lesson, Rom. ii. *unto the end.*

At the Communion.
Lætatus sum. Psalm cxxii.
I WAS glad when they said unto me . . . . . [&c.]

The Collect.
ALMIGHTY God, which madest thy blessed Son to be circumcised and obedient to the law for man: grant us the true circumcision of thy Spirit: that our hearts, and all our members, being mortified from all worldly and carnal lusts, may in all things obey thy blessed will, through the same thy Son Jesus Christ our Lord.

The Epistle. Rom. iv. Blessed is that man to whom the Lord . . . . . [&c.]
[i.e. Rom. iv. verse 8 to verse 15.]

The Gospel. Luc. ii. And it fortuned, as soon as the angels were gone . . . . . [&c.]
[i.e. Luke ii. verse 15 to verse 22.]

¶ *At Evensong.*
The first lesson, Deute. x. "And now Israel," *unto the end.*
The second lesson, Coloss. ii. *unto the end.*

The Epiphany.
At Matins.
The first lesson, Esai. lx. *unto the end.*
The second lesson, Luke iii. "And it fortuned," *unto the end.*

[*At the Communion.*]
[*Cantate Domino.*] Psalm xcvi.
O SING unto the Lord a new song . . . . . [&c.]

The Collect.
[O] GOD, which by the leading of a star didst manifest thy only-begotten Son to the Gentiles; Mercifully grant, that we, which know thee now by faith, may after this life have the fruition of thy glorious Godhead; through Christ our Lord.

The Epistle. Ephe. iii. For this cause I Paul, [&c.]
[i.e. Eph. iii. verse 1 to verse 13.]

The Gospel. Matt. ii. When Jesus was born, [&c.]
[i.e. Matt. ii. verse 1 to verse 13.]

At Evensong.

The first lesson, Esai. xlix. *unto the end.*
The second lesson, John ii. "After this he went down to Capernaum," *unto the end.*

The first Sunday after the Epiphany.

Usquequo Domine? Psalm xiii.
How long wilt thou forget me, O Lord . . . . . [&c.]

The Collect.

LORD, we beseech thee, mercifully to receive the prayers of thy people which call upon thee: and grant that they may both perceive and know what things they ought to do, and also have grace and power faithfully to fulfil the same.

The Epistle. Roma xii. I beseech you therefore brethren . . . . [&c.]
[i.e. Rom. xii. verse 1 to verse 6.]

The Gospel. Luc. ii. The father and mother of Jesus went . . . . . [&c.]
[i.e. Luke ii. verse 41 to the end.]

¶ *The second Sunday.*

Dixit insipiens. Psalm xiiii.
THE fool hath said in his heart . . . . . [&c.]

The Collect.

ALMIGHTY and everlasting God, which dost govern all things in heaven and earth: mercifully hear the supplications of thy people, and grant us thy peace all the days of our life.

AT THE COMMUNION.   23

The Epistle. Rom. xii. Seeing that we have divers gifts . . . . . [&c.]
[i.e. Rom. xii. verse 6 to verse 16.]

The Gospel. John ii. And the third day was there a marriage in Cana . . . . . [&c.]
[i.e. John ii. verse 1 to verse 12.]

¶ *The third Sunday.*

Domine, quis habitabit? Psalm xv.
LORD, who shall dwell in thy tabernacle . . . . . [&c.]

The Collect.

ALMIGHTY and everlasting God, mercifully look upon our infirmities, and in all our dangers and necessities, stretch forth thy right hand to help and defend us, through Christ our Lord.

The Epistle. Rom. xii. Be not wise in your own opinions . . . . . [&c.]
[i.e. Rom. xii. verse 16 to the end.]

The Gospel. Math. viii. When he was come down from the mountain . . . . . [&c.]
[i.e. Matt. viii. verse 1 to verse 14.]

¶ *The fourth Sunday.*

Quare fremuerunt gentes? Psalm ii.
WHY do the heathen so furiously rage together, [&c.]

The Collect.

GOD, which knowest us to be set in the midst of so many and great dangers, that for man's frailness we cannot always stand uprightly: Grant to us the health of body and soul, that all those things which we suffer for sin, by thy help we may well pass and overcome, through Christ our Lord.

The Epistle. Rom. xiii. Let every soul submit himself . . . . . [&c.]
[i.e. Rom. xiii. verse 1 to verse 8.]

The Gospel. Math. viii. And when he entered into a ship . . . . . [&c.]
[i.e. Matt. viii. verse 23 to the end.]

¶ *The fifth Sunday.*

Exaudiat te Dominus. Psalm xx.

THE Lord hear thee in the day of trouble . . . . [&c.]

The Collect.

LORD, we beseech thee to keep thy church and household continually in thy true religion: that they which do lean only upon hope of thy heavenly grace, may evermore be defended by thy mighty power; through Christ our Lord.

The Epistle. Coloss. iii. Put upon you as the elect of God . . . . . [&c.]
[i.e. Coloss. iii. verse 12 to verse 18.]

The Gospel. Math. xiii. The kingdom of heaven is like unto . . . . . [&c.]
[i.e. Matt. xiii. verse 24 to verse 31.]

The sixth Sunday (if there be so many) shall have the same Psalm, Collect, Epistle, and Gospel, that was upon the fifth.

¶ *The Sunday called Septuagesima.*

Dominus regit. Psalm xxiii.

THE Lord is my shepherd : therefore . . . . . [&c.]

The Collect.

O LORD, we beseech thee favourably to hear the prayers of thy people; that we, which are justly punished for our offences, may be mercifully delivered by thy goodness, for the glory of thy name; through Jesu Christ our Saviour, who liveth and reigneth, &c.

AT THE COMMUNION.

The Epistle. 1 Cor. ix. Perceive ye not, how that they . . . . . [&c.]
[i.e. 1 Cor. ix. verse 24 to the end.]

The Gospel. Math. xx. The kingdom of heaven is like unto a man . . . . . [&c.]
[i.e. Matt. xx. verse 1 to verse 17.]

¶ *The Sunday called Sexagesima.*

¶ [*At the Communions.*]

Domini est terra. Psalm xxiiii.

THE earth is the Lord's, and all that therein is, the compass . . . . . [&c.]

The Collect.

LORD God, which seest that we put not our trust in any thing that we do : mercifully grant that by thy power we may be defended against all adversity, through Jesus Christ our Lord.

The Epistle. 2 Cor. xi. Ye suffer fools gladly . . . [&c.]
[i.e. 2 Cor. xi. verse 19 to verse 32.]

The Gospel. Luc. viii. When much people were gathered . . . . . [&c.]
[i.e. Luke viii. verse 4 to verse 16.]

¶ *The Sunday called Quinquagesima.*

Judica me Domine. Psalm xxvi.

BE thou my judge, O lord, for I have walked . . . [&c.]

The Collect.

O LORD, which dost teach us, that all our doings without charity are nothing worth : send thy Holy Ghost, and pour into our hearts that most excellent gift of charity, the very bond of peace and all virtues, without the which, whosoever liveth is counted dead before thee : Grant this, for thy only Son Jesus Christ's sake.

* In some copies these words are omitted.

The Epistle. 1 Cor. xiii. Though I speak with the tongues . . . . . [&c.]
[i.e. 1 Cor. xiii. verse 1 to the end.]

The Gospel. Luc. xviii. Jesus took unto him the twelve . . . . . [&c.]
[i.e. Luke xviii. verse 31 to the end.]

¶ *The first day of Lent, commonly called Ashwednesday.*

Domine ne. Psalm vi.

O LORD, rebuke me not in thine indignation . . . . [&c.]

The Collect.

ALMIGHTY and everlasting God, which hatest nothing that thou hast made, and dost forgive the sins of all them that be penitent: Create and make in us new and contrite hearts, that we worthily lamenting our sins, and knowledging our wretchedness, may obtain of thee, the God of all mercy, perfect remission and forgiveness, through Jesus Christ.

The Epistle. Joel ii. Turn you unto me with all your hearts . . . . . [&c.]
[i.e. Joel ii. verse 12 to verse 17.]

The Gospel. Math. vi. When ye fast be not sad as the hypocrites are . . . . . [&c.]
[i.e. Matt. vi. verse 16 to verse 22.]

¶ *The first Sunday in Lent.*

Beati quorum. Psalm xxxii.

BLESSED is he whose unrighteousness is forgiven; and whose . . . . . [&c.]

The Collect.

O LORD, which for our sake didst fast forty days and forty nights: Give us grace to use such abstinence, that, our flesh being subdued to the Spirit, we may ever obey thy godly motions, in righteousness and true holiness, to thy honour and glory, which livest and reignest, &c.

The Epistle. 2 Cor. vi. We as helpers exhort you that ye receive not . . . . . [&c.]
[i.e. 2 Cor. vi. verse 1 to verse 11.]

The Gospel. Math. iv. Then was Jesus led away of the Spirit . . . . . [&c.]
[i.e. Matth. iv. verse 1 to verse 12.]

¶ *The second Sunday.*

De profundis. Psalm cxxx.

OUT of the deep have I called unto thee, O Lord: Lord hear . . . . . [&c.]

The Collect.

ALMIGHTY God, which dost see that we have no power of ourselves to help ourselves : keep thou us both outwardly in our bodies, and inwardly in our souls, that we may be defended from all adversities which may happen to the body, and from all evil thoughts which may assault and hurt the soul; through Jesus Christ, &c. Amen[1].

The Epistle. 1 Thess. iv. We beseech you brethren and exhort . . . . . [&c.]
[i.e. 1 Thess. iv. verse 1 to verse 9.]

The Gospel. Math. xv. Jesus went thence . . . . [&c.]
[i.e. Matth. xv. verse 21 to verse 29.]

¶ *The third Sunday.*

Judica me Deus. Psalm xliii.

GIVE sentence with me, (O God,) and defend . . . [&c.]

The Collect.

WE beseech thee, almighty God, look upon the hearty desire[s] of thy humble servants : and stretch

---

[1] In some copies, "Amen" omitted.

forth the right hand of thy majesty, to be our defence against all our enemies : through Jesus Christ our Lord.

The Epistle. Ephe. v. Be you the followers of God ..... [&c.]
[i.e. Ephes. v. verse 1 to verse 15.]

The Gospel. Luc. xi. Jesus was casting out a devil that was dumb ..... [&c.]
[i.e. Luke xi. verse 14 to verse 26.]

¶ *The fourth Sunday.*

Deus noster refugium. Psalm xlvi.
GOD is our hope and strength : a very ..... [&c.]

The Collect.

GRANT, we beseech thee, almighty God, that we, which for our evil deeds are worthily punished : by the comfort of thy grace may mercifully be relieved, through our Lord Jesus Christ.

The Epistle. Gala. iv. Tell me, ye that desire, [&c.]
[i.e. Gal. iv. verse 21 to the end.]

The Gospel. John vi. Jesus departed over the sea of Galilee ..... [&c.]
[i.e. John vi. verse 1 to verse 15.]

¶ *The fifth Sunday.*

Deus, in nomine tuo. Psalm liv.
SAVE me, (O God,) for thy Name's sake ..... [&c.]

The Collect.

WE beseech thee, almighty God, mercifully to look upon thy people : that by thy great goodness, they may be governed and preserved evermore, both in body and soul : through Jesus Christ our Lord.

AT THE COMMUNION.   29

The Epistle. Hebrues ix. Christ being an high-priest ..... [&c.]
[i.e. Heb. ix. verse 11 to verse 16.]

The Gospel. John viii. Which of you can rebuke me of sin ..... [&c.]
[i.e. John viii. verse 46 to the end.]

The Sunday next before Easter.
Exaudi deus deprecationem. Psalm lxi.
HEAR my crying, O God ..... [&c.]

The Collect.
ALMIGHTY and everlasting God, which of thy tender love toward man, has sent our Saviour Jesus Christ to take upon him our flesh, and to suffer death upon the cross, that all mankind should follow the example of his great humility: mercifully grant, that we both follow the example of his patience, and be made partakers of his resurrection: through the same Jesus Christ our Lord.

The Epistle. Philip. ii. Let the same mind be in you ..... [&c.]
[i.e. Phil. ii. verse 5 to verse 12.]

The Gospel. Math. xxvi. and xxvii. And it came to pass ..... [&c.]
[i.e. Matt. xxvi. verse 1 to chap. xxvii. verse 57.]

Monday before Easter.

The Epistle. Esai. lxiii. What is he this that cometh ..... [&c.]
[i.e. Esai. lxiii. verse 1 to the end.]

The Gospel. Mar. xiv. After two days was Easter and the dayes ..... [&c.]
[i.e. Mark xiv. verse 1 to the end.]

¶ *Tuesday before Easter.*

The Epistle. Esai. l. The Lord God hath opened mine ear ..... [&c.]

[i.e. Esai. l. verse 5 to the end.]

The Gospel. Mar. xv. And anon in the dawning the high priests ..... [&c.]

[i.e. Mark xv. verse 1 to the end.]

¶ *Wednesday before Easter.*

¶ *At the Communion.*

The Epistle. Hebr. ix. Whereas is a testament there must also ..... [&c.]

[i.e. Hebr. ix. verse 16 to the end.]

The Gospel. Luc. xxii. The feast of sweet bread which is called Easter ..... [&c.]

[i.e. Luke xxii. verse 1 to the end.]

¶ *At Evensong.*

The first lesson, Lamenta. i. *unto the end.*

¶ *Thursday before Easter.*

¶ *At Matins.*

The first lesson, Lamenta. ii. *unto the end.*

The Epistle. 1 Cor. xi. This I warn you of and commend not that .... [&c.]

[i.e. 1 Cor. xi. verse 17 to the end.]

The Gospel. Luc. xxiii. The whole multitude of them ..... [&c.]

[i.e. Luke xxiii. ver. 1 to the end.]

At Evensong.

The first lesson, Lamenta. iii. *unto the end.*

AT THE COMMUNION. 31

On Good Friday.

At Matins.

The first lesson, Gen. xxii. *unto the end.*

The Collect.

ALMIGHTY God, we beseech thee graciously to behold this thy family: for the which our Lord Jesus Christ was contented to be betrayed, and given up into the hands of wicked men, and to suffer death upon the cross: who liveth and reigneth, &c.

At the Communion.

Deus, deus meus. Psalm xxii.

My God, my God, (look upon me) . . . . . [&c.]

¶ *After the two Collects at the Communion, shall be said these two Collects following.*

The Collect.

ALMIGHTY and everlasting God, by whose Spirit the whole body of the Church is governed and sanctified: receive our supplications and prayers, which we offer before thee for all estates of men in thy holy congregation, that every member of the same, in his vocation and ministry, may truly and godly serve thee: through our Lord Jesus Christ.

MERCIFUL God, who hast made all men, and hatest nothing that thou hast made, nor wouldest the death of a sinner, but rather that he should be converted and live: Have mercy upon all Jews, Turks, Infidels, and Heretics, and take from them all ignorance, hardness of heart, and contempt of thy word: and so fetch them home, blessed Lord, to thy flock, that they may be saved among the remnant of the true Israelites, and be made one fold under one shepherd, Jesus Christ our Lord: who liveth and reigneth, &c.

The Epistle. Heb. x. The law which hath but a shadow ..... [&c.]
[i.e. Heb. x. verse 1 to verse 26.]

The Gospel. John xviii. When Jesus had spoken these words ..... [&c.]
[i.e. John xviii. verse 1 to end of chap. xix.]

At Evensong.

¶ The first lesson, Esai. liii. *unto the end.*

Easter Even.
At Matins.

¶ The first lesson, Lamenta. iv. v. *unto the end.*

At the Communion.
Domine deus salutis, Psal. lxxxviii.

O LORD God of my salvation ..... [&c.]
The Epistle. 1 Pet. iii. It is better ..... [&c.]
[i.e. 1 Pet. iii. verse 17 to the end.]

The Gospel. Matt. xxvii. When the even .. [&c.]
[i.e. Matt. xxvii. verse 57 to the end.]

¶ *Easter day.*

In the morning afore Matins, the people being assembled in the church: these Anthems shall be first solemnly sung or said.

CHRIST rising again from the dead, now dieth not. Death from henceforth hath no power upon him. For in that he died, he died but once to put away sin: but in that he liveth, he liveth unto God. And so likewise, count yourselves dead unto sin, but living unto God in Christ Jesus our Lord. Alleluia, Alleluia.

CHRIST is risen again, the firstfruits of them that sleep : for seeing that by man came death, by man also cometh the resurrection of the dead. For as by Adam all men do die, so by Christ all men shall be restored to life. Alleluia.

The Priest.
¶ Shew forth to all nations the glory of God.
The Answer.
¶ And among all people his wonderful works.

Let us pray.

O GOD, who for our redemption didst give thine only begotten Son to the death of the cross: and by his glorious resurrection hast delivered us from the power of our enemy: Grant us so to die daily from sin, that we may evermore live with him in the joy of his resurrection: through the same Christ our Lord. Amen.

¶ *Proper Psalms and Lessons.*

At Matins.
Psalms ii. lvii. cxi.
The first lesson, Exo. xii. *unto the end.*
The second lesson, Roma. vi. *unto the end.*

At the first Communion.
Conserva me domine. Psalm xvi.
PRESERVE me O God: for in thee . . . . . [&c.]

The Collect.

ALMIGHTY God, which through thy only begotten Son Jesus Christ, hast overcome death, and opened unto us the gate of everlasting life: we humbly beseech thee, that as by thy special grace, preventing us, thou dost put in our minds good desires; so by thy continual help, we may bring the same to good effect, through Jesus Christ our Lord: who liveth and reigneth, &c. Amen[n].

The Epistle. Coloss. iii. If ye be risen again with Christ . . . . . [&c.]
[i.e. Col. iii. verse 1 to verse 8.]

[n] In some copies, "Amen" omitted.

The Gospel. John xx. The first day of the Sabbaths ..... [&c.]
[i.e. John xx. verse 1 to verse 11.]

At the second Communion.
Domine quid multiplicati? Psalm iii.

LORD, how are they increased that trouble me, [&c.]

The Collect.

ALMIGHTY Father, which hast given thy only Son to die for our sins, and to rise again for our justification: Grant us so to put away the leaven of malice and wickedness, that we may alway serve thee in pureness of living and truth, through Jesus Christ our Lord.

The Epistle. 1 Cor. v. Know ye not that a little leaven ..... [&c.]
[i.e. 1 Cor. v. verse 6 to verse 9.]

The Gospel. Mar. xvi. When the Sabbath was past ..... [&c.]
[i.e. Mark xvi. to verse 9.]

At Evensong.
¶ *Proper Psalms and Lessons.*
Psalms cxiii. cxiv. cxviii.

The second lesson, Act ii. *unto the end.*

¶ *Monday in Easter Week.*
At Matins.

The second lesson, Matt. xxviii. *unto the end.*
At the Communion.
Nonne deo [subjecta?] Psalm lxii.

MY soul truly waiteth still upon God ..... [&c.]
The Collect.

ALMIGHTY God, which through thy only begotten Son Jesus Christ, hast overcome death, and opened unto us the gate of everlasting life: we humbly beseech thee, that as by thy especial[x] grace, preventing us, thou dost put in our minds good desires[y]; so by thy continual help, we may bring the same to good effect, through Jesus Christ our Lord: who liveth and reigneth, &c.

The Epistle. Acts x. Peter opened his mouth and said..... [&c.]
[i.e. Acts x. verse 34 to verse 44.]

The Gospel. Luc. xxiv. Behold two of the disciples went..... [&c.]
[i.e. Luke xxiv. verse 13 to verse 36.]

At Evensong.

¶ The second lesson, Acts iii. *unto the end.*

¶ *Tuesday in Easter Week.*
At Matins.

The second lesson, Luke xxiv. *unto* "And behold two [of them]."

At the Communion.
Laudate pueri. Psalm cxiii.

PRAISE the Lord, (ye servants)..... [&c.]

The Collect.

ALMIGHTY Father, which hast given thy only Son to die for our sins, and to rise again for our justification: Grant us so to put away the leaven of malice and wickedness, that we may alway serve thee in pureness of living and truth, through Jesus Christ our Lord.

The Epistle. Acts xiii. Ye men and brethren... [&c.]
[i.e. Acts xiii. verse 26 to verse 42.]

The Gospel. Luc. xxiv. Jesus stood in the midst of his disciples..... [&c.]
[i.e. Luke xxiv. verse 36 to verse 49.]

At Evensong.
The second lesson, 1 Cor. xv. *unto the end.*

---

[x] In some copies, "special." [y] In some copies, "desire."

¶ *The first Sunday after Easter.*

Beatus vir. Psalm cxii.

BLESSED is the man that feareth the Lord ... [&c.]

The Collect.

ALMIGHTY Father, &c. *As at the second Communion on Easter Day.*

The Epistle. 1 John v. All that is born of God ... [&c.]
[i.e. 1 John v. verse 4 to verse 13.]

The Gospel. John xx. The same day at night ... [&c.]
[i.e. John xx. verse 19 to verse 24.]

¶ *The second Sunday after Easter.*

Deus in adjutorium. Psalm lxx.

HASTE thee, O God, to deliver me ..... [&c.]

The Collect.

ALMIGHTY God, which hast given thy holy Son to be unto us, both a sacrifice for sin, and also an example of Godly life: Give us the grace that we may always most thankfully receive that his inestimable benefit, and also daily endeavour ourselves to follow the blessed steps of his most holy life.

The Epistle. 1 Peter ii. This is thankworthy ... [&c.]
[i.e. 1 Pet. ii. verse 19 to the end.]

The Gospel. John x. Christ said to his disciple I am the good shepherd ..... [&c.]
[i.e. John x. verse 11 to verse 17.]

¶ *The third Sunday.*

Confitebimur. Psalm lxxv.

UNTO thee, (O God,) do we give thanks ..... [&c.]

The Collect.

ALMIGHTY God, which shewest to all men that be in error the light of thy truth, to the intent that they may return into the way of righteousness: Grant unto all them that be admitted into the fellowship of Christ's religion, that they may eschew those things that be contrary to their profession, and follow all such things as be agreeable to the same: through our Lord Jesus Christ.

The Epistle. 1 Peter ii. Dearly beloved, I beseech you . . . . . [&c.]
[i.e. 1 Pet. ii. verse 11 to verse 18.]

The Gospel. John xvi. Jesus said to his disciples After a while . . . . . [&c.]
[i.e. John xvi. verse 6 to verse 23.]

¶ *The fourth Sunday.*

Deus stetit in synagoga. Psalm lxxxiii.
GOD standeth in the congregation of princes... [&c.]

The Collect.

ALMIGHTY God, which dost make the minds of all faithful men to be of one will: grant unto thy people, that they may love the thing, which thou commandest, and desire that which thou dost promise, that among the sundry and manifold changes of the world, our hearts may surely there be fixed, where as true joys are to be found: through Christ our Lord.

The Epistle. James i. Every good gift . . . . . [&c.]
[i.e. James i. verse 17 to verse 22.]

The Gospel. John xvi. Jesus said unto his disciples . . . . . [&c.]
[i.e. John xvi. verse 5 to verse 15.]

¶ *The fifth Sunday.*

Quam dilecta tabernacula. Psalm lxxxiv.
O HOW amiable are thy dwellings . . . . . [&c.]

The Collect.

LORD, from whom all good things do come; grant us thy humble servants, that by thy holy inspiration we may think those things that be good, and by thy merciful guiding may perform the same; through our Lord Jesus Christ.

The Epistle. James i. See that ye be doers of the word . . . . . [&c.]
[i.e. James i. verse 22 to the end.]

The Gospel. John xvi. Verily, verily I say unto you . . . . . [&c.]
[i.e. John xvi. verse 23 to the end.]

¶ *The Ascension Day.*

¶ *Proper Psalms and Lessons.*

At Matins.

Psalms viii. xv. xxi.
The second Lesson, John xiv. *unto the end.*

¶ *At the Communion.*

Omnes gentes plaudite. Psalm xlvii.

O CLAP your hands together, (all ye people) . . . [&c.]

The Collect.

GRANT, we beseech thee, almighty God, that like as we do believe thy only begotten Son our Lord to have ascended into the heavens: so we may also in heart and mind thither ascend, and with him continually dwell.

The Epistle. Acts i. In the former treatise . . . [&c.]
[i.e. Acts i. verse 1 to verse 12.]

The Gospel. Mar. xvi. Jesus appeared unto the eleven . . . . . [&c.]
[i.e. Mark xvi. verse 14 to the end.]

¶ *Proper Psalms and Lessons at Evensong.*

Psalms xxiv. lxviii. cxlviii.

The second lesson, Ephe. iv. *unto the end.*

¶ *The Sunday after the Ascension.*

Dominus regnavit. Psalm xciii.

THE lord is king, and hath put on glorious apparel..... [&c.]

The Collect.

O GOD, the King of glory, which hast exalted thine only Son Jesus Christ, with great triumph unto thy kingdom in heaven: we beseech thee leave us not comfortless, but send to us thine Holy Ghost to comfort us, and exalt us unto the same place, whither our Saviour Christ is gone before; who liveth and reigneth, &c.

The Epistle. 1 Peter iv. The end of all things is at hand..... [&c.]

[i.e. 1 Pet. iv. verse 7 to verse 12.]

The Gospel. John xv., John xvi. When the Comforter is come..... [&c.]

[i.e. John xv. verse 26, and chap. xvi. to end of verse 4.]

¶ *Whit-Sunday.*

¶ *Proper Psalms and Lessons at Matins.*
Psalms xlviii. lxvii. cxlv.

The second lesson, Act. x. "Then Peter opened his mouth," *unto the end.*

¶ *At the Communion.*

Exultate justi in Domino. Psalm xxxiii.

REJOICE in the Lord, O ye righteous..... [&c.]

The Collect.

GOD, which as upon this day hast taught the hearts of thy faithful people, by the sending to them the light of thy Holy Spirit: Grant us by the same Spirit to have a right judgment in all things, and evermore to rejoice in his holy comfort, through the merits of

Christ Jesus our Saviour, who liveth and reigneth with thee in the unity of the same Spirit one God, world without end. Amen.

The Epistle. Acts ii. When the fifty days were come ..... [&c.]
[i.e. Acts ii. verse 1 to verse 12.]

The Gospel. John xiv. Jesus said unto his disciples ..... [&c.]
[i.e. John xiv. verse 15 to verse 22.]

¶ *Proper Psalms and Lessons at Evensong.*

Psalms civ. cxlv.

The second lesson, Acts xix. "It fortuned when Apollo went to Corinthum," *unto* "After these things."

¶ *Monday in Whitsun-week.*

Jubilate Deo. Psalm c.

O BE joyful in the Lord, (all ye lands) ..... [&c.]

The Collect.

¶ GOD, which, &c., *as upon Whit-Sunday.*

The Epistle. Act. x. Then Peter opened his mouth and said ..... [&c.]
[i.e. Acts x. verse 34 to the end.]

The Gospel. John iii. So God loved the world, [&c.]
[i.e. John iii. verse 16 to verse 22.]

¶ *Tuesday.*

¶ [*At the Communion.*]

Misericordiam. Psalm ci.

MY song shall be of mercy and judgment .... [&c.]

The Collect.

GOD, which, &c., *as upon Whit-Sunday.*

The Epistle. Acts viii. When the Apostles which were at Jerusalem ..... [&c.]
[i.e. Acts viii. verse 14 to verse 18.]

The Gospel. John x. Verily, verily I say unto you..... [&c.]
[i.e. John x. verse 1 to verse 11.]

¶ *Trinity Sunday.*

¶ *At Matins.*

The first lesson, Gene. xviii. *unto the end.*
The second lesson, Math. iii. *unto the end.*

¶ *At the Communion.*

Deus misereatur. Psalm lxvii.
GOD be merciful unto us, and bless us..... [&c.]

The Collect.

ALMIGHTY and everlasting God, which hast given unto us thy servants grace by the confession of a [1] true faith to acknowledge the glory of the eternal Trinity, and in the power of the divine majesty to worship [2] the Unity: We beseech thee that through the steadfastness of this faith, we may evermore be defended from all adversity: which livest and reignest, one God, world without end. Amen.

The Epistle. Apoca. iv. After this I looked, and behold..... [&c.]
[i.e. Apoc. iv. verse 1 to the end.]

The Gospel. John iii. There was a man of the Pharisees..... [&c.]
[i.e. John iii. verse 1 to verse 16.]

¶ *The first Sunday after Trinity Sunday.*

Beati immaculati. Ps. cxix. [v. 1—8.]
BLESSED are those that be undefiled in the way, [&c.]

[1] In some copies, "of true faith."
[2] In some copies, "to worship thee in unity."

The Collect.

GOD, the strength of all them that trust in thee, mercifully accept our prayers; and because the weakness of our mortal nature can do no good thing without thee, grant us the help of thy grace, that in keeping of thy commandments, we may please thee both in will and deed; through Jesus Christ our Lord.

The Epistle. 1 John iv. Dearly beloved, let us love one another . . . . . [&c.]
[i.e. 1 John iv. verse 7 to the end.]

The Gospel. Luc. xvi. There was a certain rich man . . . . . [&c.]
[i.e. Luke xvi. verse 19 to the end.]

¶ *The Second Sunday.*

In quo corriget. Psalm cxix. [v. 9—16.]
WHEREWITHAL shall a young man cleanse his way . . . . . [&c.]

The Collect.

LORD, make us to have a perpetual fear and love of thy holy name: for thou never failest to help and govern them whom thou dost bring up in thy steadfast love. Grant this, &c.

The Epistle. 1 John iii. Marvel not, my brethren though the world . . . . . [&c.]
[i.e. 1 John iii. verse 13 to the end.]

The Gospel. Luke xiv. A certain man ordained a great supper . . . . . [&c.]
[i.e. Luke xiv. verse 16 to verse 25.]

¶ *The third Sunday.*

Retribue servo tuo. Psalm cxix. [v. 17—24.]
O DO well unto thy servant: that I may live .. [&c.]

The Collect.

LORD, we beseech thee mercifully to hear us, and unto whom thou hast given an hearty desire to pray,

AT THE COMMUNION.   43

grant that by thy mighty aid we may be defended: through Jesu[s] Christ our Lord.

The Epistle. 1 Peter v. Submit yourselves every man . . . . .   [&c.]
[1 Peter v. verse 5 to verse 12.]

The Gospel. Luc. xv. Then resorted unto him . . . [&c.]
[i.e. Luke xv. verse 1 to verse 11.]

¶ *The fourth Sunday.*
¶ *At the Communion.*

Adhesit pavimento anima. Psalm cxix. [v. 25—32.]
MY soul cleaveth to the dust : O quicken thou me . . . . .   [&c.]

The Collect.

GOD, the Protector of all that trust in thee, without whom nothing is strong, nothing is holy: increase and multiply upon us thy mercy, that thou being our ruler and guide, we may so pass through things temporal, that we finally lose not the things eternal: Grant this, heavenly Father, for Jesus Christ's sake our Lord.

The Epistle. Roma. viii. I suppose that the afflictions . . . . .   [&c.]
[i.e. Rom. viii. verse 18 to verse 24.]

The Gospel. Luc. vi. Be ye merciful, as your Father . . . . .   [&c.]
[i.e. Luke vi. verse 36 to verse 43.]

¶ *The fifth Sunday.*

Legem pone. Psalm cxix. [v. 33—40.]
TEACH me, O Lord, the way of thy statutes . . . [&c.]

The Collect.

GRANT Lord, we beseech thee, that the course of this world may be so peaceably ordered by thy governance : that thy congregation may joyfully serve thee in all godly quietness : through Jesus Christ our Lord.

The Epistle. 1 Peter iii. Be you all of one mind and of one heart . . . . . [&c.]
[i.e. 1 Peter iii. verse 8 to verse 16.]

The Gospel. Luc. v. It came to pass that . . . [&c.]
[i.e. Luke v. verse 1 to verse 12.]

¶ *The sixth Sunday.*

Et veniat super me. Psalm cxix. [v. 41—48.]
LET thy loving mercy come also unto me .. [&c.]

The Collect.

GOD, which hast prepared to them that love thee, such good things as pass all man's understanding : Pour into our hearts such love toward thee, that we loving thee in all things, may obtain thy promises, which exceed all that we can desire ; Through Jesus Christ our Lord.

The Epistle. Roma. vi. Know ye not, that all we which are baptized . . . . . [&c.]
[i.e. Rom. vi. verse 3 to verse 12.]

The Gospel. Mat. v. Jesus said unto his disciples Except your righteousness . . . . . [&c.]
[i.e. Mat. v. verse 20 to verse 27.]

¶ *The seventh Sunday.*

Memor esto. Psalm cxix. [v. 49—56.]
O THINK upon thy servant, as concerning thy word . . . . . [&c.]

The Collect.

LORD of all power and might, which art the author and giver of all good things : graff in our hearts the love of thy name, increase in us true religion, nourish us with all goodness, and of thy great mercy keep us in the same : Through Jesus Christ our Lord.

The Epistle. Roma. vi. I speak grossly, because of the infirmity ..... [&c.]
[i.e. Rom. vi. verse 19 to the end.]

The Gospel. Mar. viii. In those days, when there was ..... [&c.]
[i.e. Mark viii. verse 1 to verse 10.]

¶ *The eighth Sunday.*

¶ *At the Communion.*

Portio mea Domine. Psalm cxix. [v. 57—64.]

THOU art my portion, O Lord ..... [&c.]

The Collect.

God, whose providence is never deceived, we humbly beseech thee, that thou wilt put away from us all hurtful things, and give those things which be profitable for us: through Jesus Christ our Lord.

The Epistle. Roma. viii. Brethren, we are debtors not to the flesh ..... [&c.]
[i.e. Rom. viii. verse 12 to verse 18.]

The Gospel. Mat. vii. Beware of false prophets which come ..... [&c.]
[i.e. Matt. vii. verse 15 to verse 22.]

¶ *The ninth Sunday.*

Bonitatem. Psalm cxix. [v. 65—72.]

O LORD, thou hast dealt graciously with thy servant ..... [&c.]

The Collect.

GRANT to us, Lord, we beseech thee, the spirit to think and do always such things as be rightful: that we, which cannot be without thee, may by thee be able to live according to thy will: Through Jesus Christ our Lord.

The Epistle. 1 Cor. x. Brethren, I would not that ..... [&c.]
[i.e. 1 Cor. x. verse 1 to verse 14.]

The Gospel. Luc. xvi. Jesus said unto his disciples ..... [&c.]
[i.e. Luke xvi. verse 1 to verse 10.]

The tenth Sunday.

Manus tuæ. Psalm cxix. [v. 73—80.]
THY hands have made me and fashioned me ... [&c.]

The Collect.

LET thy merciful ears, O Lord, be open to the prayers of thy humble servants: and that they may obtain their petitions, make them to ask such things as shall please thee: Through Jesus Christ our Lord.

The Epistle. 1 Cor. xii. Concerning spiritual things ..... [&c.]
[i.e. 1 Cor. xii. verse 1 to verse 12.]

The Gospel. Luc. xix. And when he was come near ..... [&c.]
[i.e. Luke xix. verse 41 to verse 47.]

The eleventh Sunday.

Defecit. Psalm cxix. [v. 81—88.]
MY soul hath longed for thy salvation ..... [&c.]

The Collect.

GOD, which declarest thy almighty power, most chiefly in shewing mercy and pity: Give unto us abundantly thy grace, that we running to thy promises, may be made partakers of thy heavenly treasure: through Jesus Christ our Lord.

The Epistle. 1 Cor. xv. Brethren, as pertaining to the Gospel ..... [&c.]
[i.e. 1 Cor. xv. verse 1 to verse 12.]

The Gospel. Luc. xviii. Christ told this parable, [&c.]
[i.e. Luke xviii. verse 9 to verse 15.]

AT THE COMMUNION.

The twelfth Sunday.

In eternum Domine.   Psalm cxix. [v. 89—96.]
O LORD, thy word : endureth for ever . . . . .   [&c.]

The Collect.

ALMIGHTY and everlasting God, which art always more ready to hear than we to pray; and art wont to give more than either we desire or deserve : Pour down upon us the abundance of thy mercy, forgiving us those things whereof our conscience is afraid, and giving unto us that that our prayer dare not presume to ask; through Jesus Christ our Lord.

The Epistle. 2 Cor. iii. Such trust have we through Christ . . . . .   [&c.]
    [i.e. 2 Cor. iii. verse 4 to verse 10.]

The Gospel. Mar. vii. Jesus departed from the coasts . . . . .   [&c.]
    [i.e. Mark vii. verse 31 to the end.]

The thirteenth Sunday.

Quomodo dilexi.   Psalm cxix. [v. 97—104.]
LORD, what love have I unto thy law . . . . .   [&c.]

The Collect.

ALMIGHTY and merciful God, of whose only gift it cometh, that thy faithful people do unto thee true and laudable service : grant, we beseech thee, that we may so run to thy heavenly promises, that we fail not finally to attain the same : through Jesus Christ our Lord.

The Epistle. Gala. iii. To Abraham and his seed, [&c.]
    [i.e. Gal. iii. verse 16 to verse 23.]

The Gospel. Luc. x. Happy are the eyes which see . . . . .   [&c.]
    [i.e. Luke x. verse 23 to verse 38.]

The fourteenth Sunday.

Lucerna pedibus meis. Psalm cxix. [v. 105—112.]

THY word is a lantern unto my feet . . . . . [&c.]

The Collect.

ALMIGHTY and everlasting God, give unto us the increase of faith, hope, and charity: and, that we may obtain that which thou dost promise, make us to love that which thou dost command, through Jesus Christ our Lord.

The Epistle. Gala. v. I say walk in the Spirit, [&c.]
[i.e. Gal. v. verse 16 to verse 25.]

The Gospel. Luc. xvii. And it chanced as Jesus went to Jerusalem . . . . . [&c.]
[i.e. Luke xvii. verse 11 to verse 20.]

The fifteenth Sunday.

Iniquos odio habui. Psalm cxix. [v. 113—120.]

I HATE them that imagine evil things . . . . . [&c.]

The Collect.

KEEP, we beseech thee, O Lord, thy church with thy perpetual mercy, and, because the frailty of man without thee cannot but fall, keep us ever by thy help, and lead us to all things profitable to our salvation: through Jesus our Lord.

The Epistle. Gala. vi. Ye see how large a letter, [&c.]
[i.e. Gal. vi. verse 11 to the end.]

The Gospel. Matt. vi. No man can serve two masters . . . . . [&c.]
[i.e Matt. vi. verse 24 to the end.]

The sixteenth Sunday.

Feci judicium. Psalm cxix. [v. 121—128.]

I DEAL with the thing that is lawful and right... [&c.]

The Collect.

LORD, we beseech thee, let thy continual pity cleanse and defend thy congregation: and because it cannot continue in safety without thy succour, preserve it evermore by thy help and goodness; through Jesus Christ our Lord.

The Epistle. Ephes. iii. I desire that you faint not ..... [&c.]
[i.e. Ephes. iii. verse 13 to the end.]

The Gospel. Luc. vii. And it fortuned that Jesus, [&c.]
[i.e. Luke vii. verse 11 to verse 18.]

¶ The seventeenth Sunday.

Mirabilia. Psalm cxix. [v. 129—136.]

THY testimonies are wonderful: therefore ... [&c.]

The Collect.

LORD, we pray thee that thy grace may always prevent and follow us, and make us continually to be given to all good works; through Jesus Christ our Lord.

The Epistle. Ephes. iv. I (which am a prisoner of the Lord's) ..... [&c.]
[i.e. Ephes. iv. verse 1 to verse 7.]

The Gospel. Luc. xiv. It chanced that Jesus went ..... [&c.]
[i.e. Luke xiv. verse 1 to verse 12.]

¶ *The eighteenth Sunday.*

Justus es domine.   Psalm cxix. [v. 137—144.]
RIGHTEOUS art thou, O Lord : and true .... [&c.]

The Collect.

LORD, we beseech thee, grant thy people grace to avoid the infections of the devil, and with pure heart and mind to follow thee, the only God : Through Jesus Christ our Lord.

The Epistle.   1 Cor. i. I thank my God always, [&c.]
[i.e. 1 Cor. i. verse 4 to verse 9.]

The Gospel.   Math. xxii. When the Pharisees had heard . . . . . [&c.]
[i.e. Matt. xxii. verse 34 to the end.]

¶ *The nineteenth Sunday.*

Clamavi.   Psalm cxix. [v. 145—152.]
I CALL with my whole heart : hear me .... [&c.]

The Collect.

O GOD, forasmuch as without thee we are not able to please thee : Grant that the working of thy mercy may in all things direct and rule our hearts : Through Jesus Christ our Lord.

The Epistle.   Ephe. iv. This I say and testify through the Lord . . . . . [&c.]
[i.e. Ephes. iv. verse 17 to the end.]

The Gospel.   Mat. ix. Jesus entered into a ship, [&c.]
[i.e. Matt. ix. verse 1 to verse 9.]

The twentieth Sunday.

Vide humilitatem meam.   Psalm cxix. [v. 153—160.]
O CONSIDER mine adversity, and deliver me ... [&c.]

The Collect.

ALMIGHTY and merciful God, of thy bountiful goodness, keep us from all things that may hurt us : that we being ready both in body and soul, may with free hearts accomplish those things, that thou wouldest have done ; through Jesus Christ our Lord.

The Epistle. Ephe. v. Take heed therefore how ye walk . . . . . [&c.]
[i.e. Ephes. v. verse 15 to verse 22.]

The Gospel. Math. xxii. Jesus said to his disciples, the kingdom of heaven . . . . . [&c.]
[i.e. Matt. xxii. verse 1 to verse 15.]

¶ *The twenty-first Sunday.*

Principes persecuti. Psalm cxix. [v. 161—168.]
PRINCES have persecuted me without cause . . . [&c.]

The Collect.

GRANT, we beseech thee, merciful Lord, to thy faithful people, pardon and peace ; that they may be cleansed from all their sins, and serve thee with a quiet mind : Through Jesus Christ our Lord.

The Epistle. Ephe. vi. My brethren, be strong, [&c.]
[i.e. Eph. vi. verse 10 to verse 21.]

The Gospel. John iv. There was a certain ruler, [&c.]
[i.e. John iv. verse 46 to the end.]

¶ *The twenty-second Sunday.*

Appropinquet deprecatio. Psalm cxix. [v. 169—176.]
LET my complaint come before thee, O Lord, [&c.]

The Collect.

LORD, we beseech thee to keep thy household the church in continual godliness : that through thy protection, it may be free from all adversities, and devoutly given to serve thee in good works, to the glory of thy name: Through Jesus Christ our Lord.

The Epistle. Phil. i. I thank my God with all remembrance of you . . . . . [&c.]
[i.e. Phil. i. verse 3 to verse 12.]

The Gospel. Math. xviii. Peter said unto Jesus, [&c.]
[i.e. Matt. xviii. verse 21 to the end.]

¶ *The twenty-third Sunday.*

Nisi quia dominus. Psalm cxxiv.
IF the Lord himself had not been on our side, [&c.]

The Collect.
GOD our refuge and strength, which art the author of all godliness, be ready to hear the devout prayers of thy church: and grant that those things which we ask faithfully, we may obtain effectually: through Jesu [b] Christ our Lord.

The Epistle. Phil. iii. Brethren, be followers together . . . . . [&c.]
[i.e. Phil. iii. verse 17 to the end.]

The Gospel. Math. xxii. Then the Pharisees went out and took counsel . . . . . [&c.]
[i.e. Matt. xxii. verse 15 to verse 23.]

¶ *The twenty-fourth Sunday.*

Qui confidunt. Psalm cxxv.
THEY that put their trust in the Lord . . . . . [&c.]

The Collect.
LORD, we beseech thee, assoil thy people from their offences: that through thy bountiful goodness, we

---

[b] In some copies, "Jesus."

may be delivered from the bands of all those sins, which by our frailty we have committed: Grant this, &c.

The Epistle. Coloss. i. We give thanks to God, [&c.]
[i.e. Colos. i. verse 3 to verse 13.]

The Gospel. Math. ix. While Jesus spake unto the people..... [&c.]
[i.e. Matt. ix. verse 18 to verse 27.]

¶ *The twenty-fifth Sunday.*

Nisi dominus. Psalm cxxvii.

EXCEPT the Lord build the house: their labour, [&c.]

The Collect.

STIR up, we beseech thee, O Lord, the wills of thy faithful people, that they plenteously bringing forth the fruit of good works, may of thee be plenteously rewarded: through Jesus Christ our Lord.

The Epistle. Jere. xxiii. Behold, the time cometh..... [&c.]
[i.e. Jer. xxiii. verse 5 to verse 9.]

The Gospel. John vi. When Jesus lift up his eyes..... [&c.]
[i.e. John vi. verse 5 to verse 15.]

Saint Andrew's Day.

At the Communion.

Sepe expugnaverunt. Psalm cxxix.

MANY a time have they fought against me... [&c.]

The Collect.

ALMIGHTY God, which hast given such grace to thy Apostle saint Andrewe, that he counted the sharp and painful death of the cross to be an high honour, and a great glory: Grant us to take and esteem all troubles and adversities which shall come unto us for thy sake, as things profitable for us toward the obtaining of everlasting life: through Jesus Christ our Lord.

The Epistle.   Roma. x. If thou knowledge with thy mouth ....   [&c.]
[i.e. Rom. x. verse 9 to the end.]

The Gospel.   Math. iv. As Jesus walked by the sea of Galilee .....   [&c.]
[i.e. Matt. iv. verse 18 to verse 23.]

Saint Thomas the Apostle.

At the Communion [c].

Beati omnes.   Psalm cxxviii.
BLESSED are all they that fear the Lord ..... [&c.]

The Collect.

ALMIGHTY everliving [d] God, which for the more confirmation of the faith, didst suffer thy holy apostle Thomas to be doubtful in thy Son's resurrection: Grant us so perfectly, and without all doubt, to believe in thy Son Jesus Christ, that our faith in thy sight never be reproved: hear us, O Lord, through the same Jesus Christ; to whom with thee and the Holy Ghost be all honour, &c.

The Epistle. Ephes. ii. Now ye are not strangers, [&c.]
[i.e. Ephes. ii. verse 19 to the end.]

The Gospel.   John xx. Thomas one of the twelve which ....   [&c.]
[i.e. John xx. verse 24 to the end.]

¶ *The Conversion of Saint Paul.*

At Matins.

The second lesson, Acts xxii. *unto,* "They heard him."

---

[c] In some copies these words are omitted. "Almighty everlasting God."

[d] In some copies,

Confitebor tibi. Psalm cxxxviii.
I WILL give thanks unto thee, O Lord . . . . . [&c.]

The Collect.

GOD, which hast taught all the world, through the preaching of thy blessed Apostle Saint Paul: grant we beseech thee, that we which have his wonderful conversion in remembrance, may follow and fulfil the holy doctrine that he taught: through Jesus Christ our Lord.

The Epistle. Acts ix. And Saul yet breathing out . . . . . [&c.]
[i.e. Acts ix. verse 1 to verse 23.]

The Gospel. Math. xix. Peter answered and said . . . . . [&c.]
[i.e. Matt. xix. verse 27 to the end.]

¶ *At Evensong.*

¶ The second lesson, Acts xxvi. *unto the end.*

¶ *The Purification of Saint Mary the virgin.*

Ecce nunc benedicite. Psalm cxxxiv.
BEHOLD (now), praise the Lord . . . . . [&c.]

The Collect.

ALMIGHTY and everlasting God, we humbly beseech thy Majesty, that as thy only begotten Son was this day presented in the Temple, in the substance of our flesh: so grant that we may be presented unto thee with pure and clear minds: By Jesus Christ our Lord.

The Epistle.
The same that is appointed for the Sunday.

The Gospel. Luc. ii. When the time of their purification . . . . . [&c.]
[i.e. Luke ii. verse 22 to verse 28.]

¶ Saint Mathies day.

Eripe me. Psalm cxl.

DELIVER me, O Lord, from the evil man . . . . [&c.]

The Collect.

ALMIGHTY God, which in the place of the traitor Judas, didst choose thy faithful servant Mathie to be of the number of thy twelve Apostles : Grant that thy church being alway preserved from false Apostles, may [e] be ordered and guided by faithful and true pastors: Through Jesus Christ our Lord.

The Epistle. Acts i. In those days Peter stood up . . . . . [&c.]
[i.e. Acts i. verse 15 to the end.]

The Gospel. Math. xi. In that time Jesus answered . . . . . [&c.]
[i.e. Matt. xi. verse 25 to the end.]

The Annunciation of the virgin Mary.

Domine, non est exal. Psalm cxxxi.

LORD, I am not high-minded . . . . . [&c.]

The Collect.

WE beseech thee, Lord, pour thy grace into our hearts, that as we have known Christ thy Son's incarnation, by the message of an Angel ; so by his cross and passion, we may be brought unto the glory of his resurrection : Through the same Christ our Lord.

The Epistle. Esai. vii. God spake once again unto Ahaz . . . . . [&c.]
[i.e. Isai. vii. verse 10 to verse 16.]

The Gospel. Luc. i. And in the sixth month the angel Gabriel . . . . . [&c.]
[i.e. Luke i. verse 26 to verse 39.]

[e] In some copies, "and may."

¶ *Saint Mark's Day.*

Domine clamavi. Psalm cxli.

LORD, I call upon thee, haste thee unto me .. [&c.]

The Collect.

ALMIGHTY God, which hast instructed thy holy Church with the heavenly doctrine of thy Evangelist Saint Mark: give us grace so to be established by thy holy gospel, that we be not, like children, carried away with every blast of vain doctrine: Through Jesus Christ our Lord.

The Epistle. Ephes. iv. Unto every one of us is given grace ..... [&c.]
[i.e. Eph. iv. verse 7 to verse 17.]

The Gospel. John xv. I am the true vine ... [&c.]
[i.e. John xv. verse 1 to verse 12.]

¶ *Saint Philip and James.*

¶ *At Matins.*

The second lesson, Acts viii. *unto,* "When the apostles."

¶ *At the Communion.*

Ecce quam bonum! Psalm cxxxiii.

BEHOLD, how good and joyful a thing it is ... [&c.]

The Collect.

ALMIGHTY God, whom truly to know is everlasting life: Grant us perfectly to know thy Son Jesus Christ, to be the way, the truth, and the life, as thou hast taught Saint Philip, and other the Apostles: Through Jesus Christ our Lord.

The Epistle. James i. James the servant of God, [&c.]
[i.e. James i. verse 1 to verse 13.]

The Gospel. John xiv. And Jesus said unto his disciples ..... [&c.]
[i.e. John xiv. verse 1 to verse 15.]

Saint Barnabe Apostle.

At Matins.

¶ The second lesson, Acts xiv. *unto the end.*

¶ *At the Communion.*

Voce mea ad Dominum.   Psalm cxlii.

I CRIED unto the Lord with my voice ....   [&c.]

The Collect.

LORD Almighty, which hast endued thy holy Apostle Barnabas with singular gifts of thy Holy Ghost: let us not be destitute of thy manifold gifts, nor yet of grace to use them alway to thy honour and glory: Through Jesus Christ our Lord.

The Epistle.   Act. xi. Tidings of these things came unto .....   [&c.]

[i.e. Acts xi. verse 22 to the end.]

The Gospel.   John xv. This is my commandment that ye love together .....   [&c.]

[i.e. John xv. verse 12 to verse 17.]

¶ *At Evensong.*

¶ The second lesson, Acts xv. *unto,* "After certain days."

¶ Saint John Baptist.

¶ *Proper Lessons at Matins.*

The first lesson, Malach. iii. *unto the end.*
The second lesson, Mat. iii. *unto the end.*

At the Communion.

Domine exaudi.   Psalm cxliii.

HEAR my prayer, O Lord, and consider my desire ....   [&c.]

The Collect.

ALMIGHTY God, by whose providence thy servant John Baptist was wonderfully born, and sent to prepare the way of thy Son our Saviour by preaching of penance : make us so to follow his doctrine and holy life, that we may truly repent according to his preaching, and after his example constantly speak the truth, boldly rebuke vice, and patiently suffer for the truth's sake : through Jesus Christ our Lord.

The Epistle. Esai. xl. Be of good cheer my people . . . . . [&c.]
[i.e. Isai. xl. verse 1 to verse 12.]

The Gospel. Luc. i. Elizabeth's time came . . . [&c.]
[i.e. Luke i. verse 57 to the end.]

Proper Lesson, at Evensong.
The first lesson, Malach. iv.ᶠ *unto the end.*
The second lesson, Mat. xiv. *unto,* "When Jesus heard."

¶ *Saint Peter's Day.*

At Matins.
The second lesson, Acts iii. *unto the end.*

At the Communion.
Benedictus dominus. Psalm cxliv.
BLESSED be the Lord my strength . . . . . [&c.]

The Collect.
ALMIGHTY God, which by thy Son Jesus Christ hast given to thy Apostle Saint Peter many excellent gifts, and commandedst him earnestly to feed thy flock ; make, we beseech thee, all bishops and pastors diligently to preach thy holy word, and the people obediently to follow the same, that they may receive the crown of everlasting Glory, through Jesus Christ our Lord.

The Epistle. Acts xii. At the same time, Herod the King . . . . . [&c.]
[i.e. Acts xii. verse 1 to verse 12.]

ᶠ In some copies, misprinted Malach. iii.

The Gospel. Mat. xvi. When Jesus came into the coasts . . . . . [&c.]
[i.e. Matt. xvi. verse 13 to verse 20.]

At Evensong.
The second lesson, Acts iv. *unto the end.*

¶ *Saint Mary Magdalene.*

Lauda anima mea. Psalm cxlvi.
PRAISE the Lord, O my soul . . . . . [&c.]

The Collect.
MERCIFUL Father, give us grace, that we never presume to sin through the example of any creature, but if[g] it shall chance us at any time to offend thy divine majesty, that then we may truly repent, and lament the same, after the example of Mary Magdalene, and by lively faith obtain remission of all our sins: through the only merits of thy Son our Saviour Christ.

The Epistle. Prov. xxxi. Whosoever findeth an honest faithful . . . . . [&c.]
[i.e. Prov. xxxi. verse 10 to the end.]

The Gospel. Luc. vii. And one of the Pharisees desired Jesus . . . . . [&c.]
[i.e. Luke vii. verse 36 to the end.]

¶ *Saint James the Apostle.*

Laudate Dominum de celis. Psalm cxlviii.
O PRAISE the Lord of heaven . . . . . [&c.]

The Collect.
GRANT, O merciful God, that as thine holy Apostle James leaving his father and all that he had, with-

---
[g] In some copies, "but and if."

out delay, was obedient unto the calling of thy Son Jesus Christ, and followed him: So we forsaking all worldly [h] and carnal affections, may be evermore ready to follow thy commandments: through Jesus Christ our Lord.

The Epistle. Act. xi. Acts xii. In those days came prophets from ..... [&c.]

[i.e. Acts xi. verse 27 to verse 3 of chap. xii.]

The Gospel. Math. xx. Then came to him the mother of Zebedee's children ..... [&c.]

[i.e. Matt. xx. verse 20 to verse 29.]

Saint Bartholomewe.

Non nobis domine. Psalm cxv.

NOT unto us, (O Lord,) not unto us ..... [&c.]

The Collect.

O ALMIGHTY and everlasting God, which hast given grace to thy apostle Bartholomewe truly to believe and to preach thy word: grant, we beseech thee, unto thy church, both to love that he believed, and to preach that he taught: through Christ our Lord.

The Epistle. Acts v. By the hands of the Apostles ..... [&c.]

[i.e. Acts v. verse 12 to verse 17.]

The Gospel. Luc. xxii. And there was a strife among them ..... [&c.]

[i.e. Luke xxii. verse 24 to verse 31.]

¶ Saint Mathewe.

Laudate Dominum omnes gentes. Psalm cxvii.

O PRAISE the Lord, all ye heathen ..... [&c.]

---

[h] In some copies, "all the worldly."

The Collect.

ALMIGHTY God, which by thy blessed Son didst call Mathewe from the receipt of custom to be an Apostle and Evangelist: Grant us grace to forsake all covetous desires and inordinate love of riches, and to follow thy said Son Jesus Christ: who liveth and reigneth, &c.

The Epistle. 2 Cor. iv. Seeing that we have such an office ..... [&c.]
[i.e. 2 Cor. iv. verse 1 to verse 7.]

The Gospel. Math. ix. And as Jesus passed forth,[&c.]
[i.e. Matt. ix. verse 9 to verse 14.]

¶ *Saint Michael and all Angels.*

¶ *At the Communion.*

Laudate pueri. Psal. cxiii.

PRAISE the Lord, (ye servants) ..... [&c.]

The Collect.

EVERLASTING God, which hast ordained and constituted the services of all Angels and men in a wonderful order: mercifully grant, that they which alway do thee service in heaven, may by thy appointment succour and defend us in earth: through Jesus Christ our Lord, &c.

The Epistle. Apoca. xii. There was a great battle in heaven ..... [&c.]
[i.e. Apoc. xii. verse 7 to verse 13.]

The Gospel. Math. xviii. At the same time came the disciples ..... [&c.]
[i.e. Matt. xviii. verse 1 to verse 11.]

¶ *Saint Luke Evangelist.*

Super flumina. Psalm cxxxvii.

BY the waters of Babylon we sat down and wept ..... [&c.]

The Collect.

ALMIGHTY God, which calledst Luke the physician, whose praise is in the gospel, to be a physician of the soul: it may please thee by the wholesome medicines of his doctrine, to heal all the diseases of our souls: through thy Son Jesus Christ our Lord.

The Epistle. 2 Tim. iv. Watch thou in all things ..... [&c.]
[i.e. 2 Tim. iv. verse 5 to verse 16.]

The Gospel. Luc. x. The Lord appointed other seventy ..... [&c.]
[i.e. Luke x. verse 1 to verse 7.]

¶ *Symon and Jude Apostles.*

Laudate Dominum. Psalm cl.

O PRAISE God in his holiness ..... [&c.]

The Collect.

ALMIGHTY God, which hast builded the congregation upon the foundation of the Apostles and prophets, Jesu Christ himself being the head corner-stone: grant us so to be joined together in unity of spirit by their doctrine, that we may be made an holy temple acceptable to thee: through Jesu Christ our Lord.

The Epistle. Jude 1. Judas the servant of Jesus Christ ..... [&c.]
[i.e. Jude verse 1 to verse 9.]

The Gospel. John xv. This command I you .. [&c.]
[i.e. John xv. verse 17 to the end.]

¶ *All Saints.*

Proper Lessons at Matins.

The first lesson, Sapi. iii. *unto,* "Blessed is rather the Barren."

The second lesson, Hebre. xi. xii. "Saints by faith subdued," *unto,* "If ye endure chastising."

At the Communion.

Cantate Domino.   Psalm cxlix.

O SING unto the Lord a new song . . . . .   [&c.]

The Collect.

ALMIGHTY God, which hast knit together thy elect in one communion and fellowship in the mystical body of thy Son Christ our Lord; grant us grace so to follow thy holy Saints in all virtues, and godly living, that we may come to those unspeakable[1] joys, which thou hast prepared for all them that unfeignedly love thee; through Jesus Christ.

The Epistle.   Apoca. vii. Behold, I John saw another angel . . . .   [&c.]

[i.e. Apoc. vii. verse 2 to verse 13.]

The Gospel.   Math. v. Jesus seeing the people, [&c.]

[i.e. Matt. v. verse 1 to verse 13.]

¶ *Proper Lessons at Evensong.*

The first lesson, Sapi. v. *unto*, "His jealousy also."

The second lesson, Apoc. xix. *unto*, "And I saw an angel stand."

---

[1] In some copies, "inspeakable."

THE
SUPPER OF THE LORD,
AND
THE HOLY COMMUNION,
COMMONLY CALLED THE MASS.

¶ *SO many as intend to be partakers of the holy Communion, shall signify their names to the Curate over night, or else in the morning, afore the beginning of Matins*[j]*, or immediately after.*

¶ *And if any of those be an open and notorious evil liver, so that the congregation by him is offended, or have done any wrong to his neighbours by word or deed: The Curate shall call him, and advertise him, in any wise not to*[k] *presume to the Lord's table, until he have openly declared himself to have truly repented, and amended his former naughty life: that the congregation may thereby be satisfied, which afore were offended: and that he have recompensed the parties, whom he hath done wrong unto, or at the least be in full purpose so to do, as soon as he conveniently may.*

¶ *The same order shall the Curate use, with those betwixt whom he perceiveth malice and hatred to reign, not suffering them to be partakers of the Lord's table, until he know them to be reconciled. And if one of the parties so at variance be content to forgive from the bottom of his heart all that the other hath trespassed against him, and to make amends for that he himself hath offended: and the other party will not be persuaded to a godly unity, but remain still in his frowardness and malice: The Minister in that case ought to admit the penitent person to the holy Communion, and not him that is obstinate.*

¶ *Upon the day, and at the time appointed for the ministration of the holy Communion, the Priest that shall execute the holy ministry*[l]*, shall put upon him the vesture appointed*

---

[j] In some copies, "of the Matins." *omitted.*
[k] In most copies, "to" omitted.
[l] In some copies, "the ministry."

for that ministration, that is to say: a white Albe plain, with a vestment or Cope. And where there be many Priests or Deacons, there so many shall be ready to help the Priest, in the ministration, as shall be requisite: And shall have upon them likewise the vestures appointed for their ministry, that is to say, Albes with tunicles. Then shall the Clerks sing in English for the office, or Introit, (as they call it,) a Psalm appointed for that day.

The priest standing humbly afore the midst of the Altar, shall say the Lord's prayer, with this Collect.

ALMIGHTY God, unto whom all hearts be open, and all desires known, and from whom no secrets are hid: cleanse the thoughts of our hearts, by the inspiration of thy Holy Spirit: that we may perfectly love thee, and worthily magnify thy holy name: through Christ our Lord. Amen.

Then shall he say a Psalm appointed for the introit: which Psalm ended, the Priest shall say, or else the Clerks shall sing,

        iii. Lord have mercy upon us.
        iii. Christ have mercy upon us.
        iii. Lord have mercy upon us.

Then the Priest standing at God's board shall begin,

Glory be to God on high.

The Clerks. And in earth peace, good will towards men.

We praise thee, we bless thee, we worship thee, we glorify thee, we give thanks to thee for thy great glory, O Lord GOD, heavenly King, God the Father Almighty.

O Lord the only begotten Son Jesu Christ, O Lord GOD, Lamb of GOD, Son of the Father, that takest away the sins of the world, have mercy upon us: thou that takest away the sins of the world, receive our prayer.

Thou that sittest at the right hand of God the

Father, have mercy upon us: For thou only art holy, thou only art the Lord. Thou only, O Christ, with the Holy Ghost, are most high in the glory of God the Father. Amen.

Then the priest shall turn him to the people and say,
The Lord be with you.
The Answer. And with thy spirit.
The Priest. Let us pray.

Then shall follow the Collect of the day, with one of these two Collects following, for the King.

Priest. Let us pray [m].

ALMIGHTY God, whose kingdom is everlasting, and power infinite, have mercy upon the whole congregation, and so rule the heart of thy chosen servant Edward the sixth, our king and governor, that he (knowing whose minister he is) may above all things, seek thy honour and glory, and that we his subjects (duly considering whose authority he hath) may faithfully serve, honour, and humbly obey him, in thee, and for thee, according to thy blessed word and ordinance: through Jesus Christ our Lord, who with thee, and the Holy Ghost, liveth and reigneth, ever one God, world without end. Amen.

ALMIGHTY and everlasting GOD, we be taught by thy holy word, that the hearts of Kings are in thy rule and governance, and that thou dost dispose, and turn them as it seemeth best to thy godly wisdom: We humbly beseech thee so [n] to dispose and govern the heart of Edward the sixth, thy servant, our King and governor, that in all his thoughts, words, and works, he may ever seek thy honour and glory, and study to preserve thy people committed to his charge, in wealth, peace, and godliness: Grant this, O merciful Father, for thy dear Son's sake, Jesus Christ our Lord. Amen.

[m] In some copies, "*Priest.* Let us pray" *omitted.*   [n] In some copies, "so" *omitted.*

The Collects ended, the priest, or he that is appointed, shall read the Epistle, in a place assigned for the purpose, saying,

The Epistle of Saint Paul, written in the ⸺ Chapter of ⸺ to the ⸺

The Minister then shall read the Epistle. Immediately after the Epistle ended, the priest, or one appointed to read the Gospel, shall say,

The holy Gospel, written in the ⸺ Chapter of ⸺

The Clerks and people shall answer,

Glory be to thee, O Lord.

The Priest or Deacon then shall read the Gospel: After the Gospel ended, the Priest shall begin,

I BELIEVE in one God.

The Clerks shall sing the rest.

The Father almighty, maker of heaven and earth, and of all things visible, and invisible: And in one Lord Jesu Christ, the only begotten Son of God, begotten of his Father before all worlds, God of GOD, light of light, very God of very God, begotten, not made, being of one substance with the Father, by whom all things were made, who for us men, and for our salvation, came down from heaven, and was incarnate by the Holy Ghost of the Virgin Mary, and was made man, and was crucified also for us under Pontius Pilate, he suffered and was buried, and the third day he arose again according to the scriptures, and ascended into heaven, and sitteth at the right hand of the Father: and he shall come again with glory, to judge both the quick and the dead.

And I believe in the Holy Ghost, the Lord and giver of life, who proceedeth from the Father and the Son, who with the Father and the Son together, is worshipped and glorified, who spake by the prophets. And I believe one Catholic and Apostolic Church. I acknowledge one Baptism, for the remission of sins.

THE COMMUNION. 69

And I look for the resurrection of the dead: and the life of the world to come. Amen.

¶ *After the Creed ended, shall follow the Sermon or Homily, or some portion of one of the Homilies, as they shall be hereafter divided: wherein if the people be not exhorted to the worthy receiving of the holy Sacrament of the body and blood of our Saviour Christ, then shall the Curate give this exhortation, to those that be minded to receive the same.*

DEARLY beloved in the Lord, ye that mind to come to the holy Communion of the body and blood of our Saviour Christ, must consider what St. Paul writeth to the Corinthians, how he exhorteth all persons diligently to try and examine themselves, before they presume to eat of that bread and drink of that cup: for as the benefit is great, if with a truly penitent heart, and lively faith, we receive that holy Sacrament; (for then we spiritually eat º the flesh of Christ, and drink his blood, then we dwell in Christ and Christ in us, we be made one with Christ, and Christ with us;) so is the danger great, if we receive the same unworthily; for then we become guilty of the body and blood of Christ our Saviour, we eat and drink our own damnation, not considering the Lord's body. We kindle God's wrath over us, we provoke him to plague us with divers diseases, and sundry kinds of death. Therefore if any here be a blasphemer, advouterer, or be in malice, or envy, or in any other grievous crime (except he be truly sorry therefore, and earnestly minded to leave the same vices, and do trust himself to be reconciled to Almighty God, and in charity with all the world), let him bewail his sins, and not come to that holy table; lest after the taking of that most blessed bread, the devil enter into him, as he did into Judas, to fill him full of all iniquity, and bring him to destruction, both of body and soul.

º In some copies, "eat of."

Judge therefore yourselves (brethren) that ye be not judged of the Lord. Let your minds ᵖ be without desire to sin, repent you truly for your sins past, have an earnest and lively faith in Christ our Saviour, be in perfect charity with all men ; so shall ye be meet partakers of those holy mysteries. And above all things : ye must give most humble and hearty thanks to God the Father, the Son, and the Holy Ghost, for the redemption of the world by the death and passion of our Saviour Christ, both God and man, who did humble himself even to the death upon the cross, for us miserable sinners, which lay in darkness and shadow of death, that he might make us the children of God, and exalt us to everlasting life. And to the end that we should alway remember the exceeding love of our Master, and only Saviour Jesu Christ, thus dying for us, and the innumerable benefits, which (by his precious blood-shedding) he hath obtained to us, he hath left in those holy mysteries, as a pledge of his love, and a continual remembrance of the same, his own blessed body, and precious blood, for us to feed upon spiritually, to our endless comfort and consolation. To him therefore, with the Father and the Holy Ghost, let us give (as we are most bounden) continual thanks, submitting ourselves wholly to his holy will and pleasure, and studying to serve him in true holiness and righteousness, all the days of our life. Amen.

¶ *In Cathedral churches or other places, where there is daily Communion, it shall be sufficient to read this exhortation above written, once in a month. And in parish churches, upon the week days it may be left unsaid.*

¶ *And if upon the Sunday or holyday, the people be negligent to come to the Communion: Then shall the Priest earnestly exhort his parishioners, to dispose themselves to the receiving of the holy communion more diligently, saying these or like words unto them.*

ᵖ In some copies, "mend."

THE COMMUNION.

DEAR friends, and you especially upon whose souls I have cure and charge, on   next, I do intend by God's grace, to offer to all such as shall be godly disposed, the most comfortable Sacrament of the body and blood of Christ, to be taken of them in the remembrance of his most fruitful and glorious Passion : by the which passion we have obtained remission of our sins, and be made partakers of the kingdom of heaven, whereof we be assured and ascertained, if we come to the said Sacrament with hearty repentance for our offences, stedfast faith in God's mercy, and earnest mind to obey God's will, and to offend no more. Wherefore our duty is to come to these holy mysteries, with most hearty thanks to be given to Almighty GOD for his infinite mercy and benefits given and bestowed upon us his unworthy servants, for whom he hath not only given his body to death, and shed his blood, but also doth vouchsafe in a Sacrament and mystery to give us his said body and blood to feed upon spiritually. The which Sacrament being so divine and holy a thing, and so comfortable to them which receive it worthily, and so dangerous to them that will presume to take the same unworthily : My duty is to exhort you in the mean season, to consider the greatness of the thing, and to search and examine your own consciences, and that not lightly nor after the manner of dissimulers with GOD : but as they which should come to a most Godly and heavenly banquet, not to come but in the marriage garment required of God in scripture ; that you may (so much as lieth in you) be found worthy to come to such a table. The ways and means thereto is,

First, that you be truly repentant of your former evil life, and that you confess with an unfeigned heart to Almighty God your sins and unkindness towards his Majesty committed, either by will, word, or deed, infirmity or ignorance : and that with inward sorrow and tears you bewail your offences, and require of Almighty God mercy and pardon, promising to him (from the bottom of your hearts) the amendment of your former life. And amongst all others, I am commanded of God, especially to move and exhort you to reconcile yourselves to your neighbours, whom you have offended, or who hath offended you, putting out of your hearts all hatred and malice against them, and to be in love and charity with all the world, and to forgive other as you would that God should forgive you. And if any man have done wrong to any other, let him make satisfaction, and due restitution of all lands and goods, wrongfully taken away or withholden, before he come to God's board, or at the least be in full mind and purpose so to do, as soon as he is able; or else let him not come to this holy table, thinking to deceive God, who seeth all men's hearts. For neither the absolution of the priest can any thing avail them, nor the receiving of this holy sacrament doth any thing but increase their damnation. And if there be any of you, whose conscience is troubled and grieved in any thing, lacking comfort or counsel, let him come to me, or to some other discreet and learned priest, taught in the law of God, and confess and open his sin and grief secretly, that he may receive such ghostly counsel, advice, and comfort, that his conscience may be relieved, and that of us (as of the ministers of GOD and of the church) he may receive comfort and absolution, to the satisfaction of his mind, and avoiding of all scruple and doubtfulness: requiring such as shall be satisfied with a general confession, not to be offended with them that do use, to their further satisfying, the auricular and secret confession to the priest; nor those also which think needful or convenient, for the quietness of their own consciences, particularly to open their sins to the priest, to be offended with them that are satisfied with their humble confession to GOD, and the general confession to the church. But in all things to follow and keep the rule of charity, and every man to be satisfied with his own conscience, not judging other men's minds or consciences; where as he hath no warrant of God's word to the same.

¶ *Then shall follow for the Offertory one or more of these Sentences of holy scripture, to be sung whiles the people do offer, or else one of them to be said by the minister, immediately afore the offering.*

LET your light so shine before men, that they may see your good works, and glorify your Father which is in heaven. *Math.* v.

Lay not up for yourselves treasure upon the earth, where the rust and moth doth corrupt, and where thieves break through and steal: But lay up for yourselves treasure ᵠ in heaven, where neither rust nor moth doth corrupt, and where thieves do not break through nor steal. *Math.* vi.

Whatsoever you would that men should do unto you, even so do you unto them: for this is the law and the Prophets. *Math.* vii.

Not every one that saith unto me, Lord, Lord, shall enter into the kingdom of heaven, but he that doeth the will of my Father which is in heaven. *Math.* vii.

Zachee stood forth, and said unto the Lord, Behold, Lord, the half of my goods I give to the poor, and if I have done any wrong to any man, I restore fourfold. *Luc.* xix.

Who goeth a warfare at any time at his own cost? Who planteth a vineyard, and eateth not of the fruit thereof? Or who feedeth a flock, and eateth not of the milk of the flock? 1 *Cor.* ix.

If we have sown unto you spiritual things, is it a great matter if we shall reap your worldly things? 1 *Cor.* ix.

ᵠ In some copies, "treasures."

Do ye not know, that they which minister about holy things, live of the sacrifice? They which wait of the altar are partakers with the altar? Even so hath the Lord also ordained: that they which preach the Gospel, should live of the Gospel. 1 *Cor.* ix.

He which soweth little, shall reap little, and he that soweth plenteously, shall reap plenteously. Let every man do according as he is disposed in his heart; not grudgingly, or of necessity; for God loveth a cheerful giver. 2 *Cor.* ix.

Let him that is taught in the word, minister unto him that teacheth, in all good things. Be not deceived; GOD is not mocked. For whatsoever a man soweth, that shall he reap. *Gala.* vi.

While we have time, let us do good unto all men, and specially unto them, which are of the household of faith. *Gala.* vi.

Godliness is great riches, if a man be contented with that he hath: For we brought nothing into the world, neither may[r] we carry any thing out. 1 *Timo.* vi.

Charge them which are rich in this world, that they be ready to give, and glad to distribute, laying up in store[s] for themselves a good foundation, against the time to come, that they may attain eternal life. 1 *Timo.* vi.

GOD is not unrighteous, that he will forget your works and labour, that proceedeth of love, which love ye have shewed for his name's sake, which have ministered unto[t] the saints, and yet do minister. *Hebre.* vi.

To do good, and to distribute, forget not, for with such sacrifices God is pleased. *Hebre.* xiii.

Whoso hath this world's good, and seeth his brother have need, and shutteth up his compassion from him, how dwelleth the love of God in him? 1 *John* iii.

---

[r] In some copies, "can." [s] In several copies, "in store" *omitted.*
[t] In several copies, "to the."

Give alms of thy goods, and turn never thy face from any poor man, and then the face of the Lord shall not be turned away from thee. *Toby* iv.

Be merciful after thy power: if thou hast much, give plenteously; if thou hast little, do thy diligence gladly to give of that little: for so gatherest thou thyself a good reward in the day of necessity. *Toby* iv.

He that hath pity upon the poor lendeth unto the Lord; and look, what he layeth out, it shall be paid him again. *Prov.* xix.

Blessed be the man that provideth for the sick and needy; the Lord shall deliver him, in the time of trouble. *Psalm* xli.

Where there be Clerks, they shall sing one, or many of the sentences above written, according to the length and shortness of the time, that the people be offering.

In the mean time, whiles the Clerks do sing the Offertory, so many as are [a] *disposed, shall offer unto the poor men's box every one according to his ability and charitable mind. And at the offering days appointed, every man and woman shall pay to the Curate the due and accustomed offerings.*

Then so many as shall be partakers of the holy Communion, shall tarry still in the quire, or in some convenient place nigh the quire, the men on the one side, and the women on the other side. All other (that mind not to receive the said holy Communion) shall depart out of the quire, except the ministers and Clerks.

Then shall the minister take so much Bread and Wine, as shall suffice for the persons appointed to receive the holy Communion, laying the bread upon the corporas, or else in the paten, or in some other comely thing prepared for that purpose: And putting the wine into the Chalice, or else in some fair or convenient cup, prepared for that use (if the chalice will not serve), putting thereto a little pure and clean water: And setting both the bread and wine upon the Altar: then the Priest shall say,

[a] In some copies, "be."

The Lord be with you.
Answer. And with thy spirit.
Priest. Lift up your hearts.
Answer. We lift them up unto the Lord.
Priest. Let us give thanks to our Lord God.
Answer. It is meet and right so to do.
Priest[x]. It is very meet, right, and our bounden duty, that we should at all times, and in all places, give thanks to thee, O Lord, holy Father, almighty everlasting God.

¶ *Here shall follow the proper preface*[y] *according to the time (if there be any specially appointed,) or else immediately shall follow,*

Therefore with angels, &c.

PROPER PREFACES.

¶ *Upon Christmas Day.*

BECAUSE thou didst give Jesus Christ, thine only Son, to be born as this day for us, who by the operation of the Holy Ghost was made very man, of the substance of the Virgin Mary his mother, and that without spot of sin, to make us clean from all sin. Therefore &c.

¶ *Upon Easter Day.*

BUT chiefly are we bound to praise thee, for the glorious resurrection of Thy Son Jesus Christ, our Lord; for he is the very Paschal Lamb, which was offered for us, and hath taken away the sin of the world, who by his death hath destroyed death, and by his rising to life again hath restored to us everlasting life. Therefore &c.

¶ *Upon the Ascension Day.*

THROUGH thy most dear beloved Son, Jesus Christ our Lord, who after his most glorious resurrection

---

[x] In several copies, "*The Priest.*"   [y] In some copies, "Prefaces."

manifestly appeared to all his disciples, and in their sight ascended up into heaven, to prepare a place for us, that where he is, thither might we also ascend, and reign with him in glory. Therefore &c.

¶ *Upon Whitsunday.*

THROUGH Jesus Christ our Lord, according to whose most true promise, the Holy Ghost came down this day from heaven, with a sudden great sound, as it had been a mighty wind, in the likeness of fiery tongues, lighting upon the Apostles, to teach them, and to lead them to all truth, giving them both the gift of divers languages, and also boldness with fervent zeal, constantly to preach the Gospel unto all nations, whereby we are brought out of darkness and error, into the clear light and true knowledge of thee, and of thy Son Jesus Christ. Therefore &c.

¶ *Upon the feast of the Trinity.*

IT is very meet, right, and our bounden duty, that we should at all times, and in all places, give thanks to thee, O Lord almighty, everlasting God, which art one God, one Lord, not one only person, but three persons in one substance: For that which we believe of the glory of the Father, the same we believe of the Son, and of the Holy Ghost, without any difference, or inequality: whom the angels &c.

After which preface shall follow immediately,

Therefore with Angels and Archangels, and with all the holy company of heaven, we laud and magnify thy glorious name, evermore praising thee, and saying,

¶ Holy, holy, holy, Lord God of Hosts: heaven and earth are full of thy glory: Osannah in the highest. Blessed is he that cometh in the name of the Lord: Glory to thee, O Lord, in the highest.

This the Clerks shall also sing.

¶ *When the Clerks have done singing, then shall the Priest, or Deacon, turn him to the people, and say,*

Let us pray for the whole state of Christ's church.

¶ *Then the Priest, turning him to the Altar, shall say or sing, plainly and distinctly, this prayer following:*

ALMIGHTY and everliving God, which by thy holy apostle hast taught us to make prayers and supplications, and to give thanks for all men: We humbly beseech thee most mercifully to receive these our prayers, which we offer unto thy divine Majesty, beseeching thee to inspire continually the universal church with the spirit of truth, unity, and concord: And grant that all they that do confess thy holy name, may agree in the truth of thy holy word, and live in unity and godly love. Specially we beseech thee to save and defend thy servant Edward our King, that under him we may be Godly and quietly governed. And grant unto his whole council, and to all that be put in authority under him, that they may truly and indifferently minister justice, to the punishment of wickedness and vice, and to the maintenance of God's true religion and virtue. Give grace (O heavenly Father) to all Bishops, Pastors, and Curates, that they may both by their life and doctrine set forth thy true and lively word, and rightly and duly administer thy holy Sacraments: and to all thy people give thy heavenly grace, that with meek heart and due reverence they may hear and receive thy holy word, truly serving thee in holiness and righteousness all the days of their life. And we most humbly beseech thee of thy goodness (O Lord) to comfort and succour all them, which in this transitory life be in trouble, sorrow, need, sickness, or any other adversity. And especially we commend unto thy merciful goodness this congregation which is here assembled in thy name, to celebrate the commemoration of the most glorious death of thy Son: And here we do give unto thee most high praise, and hearty thanks, for the wonderful grace and virtue, declared in all thy saints, from the beginning of the world: And chiefly in the glorious and most blessed virgin Mary, mother of thy Son Jesu Christ our Lord and God, and in the holy Patriarchs, Prophets, Apostles and Martyrs, whose examples (O Lord) and stedfastness in thy faith, and keeping thy holy commandments, grant us to follow. We commend unto thy mercy (O Lord) all other thy servants, which are departed hence from us, with the sign of faith, and now do rest in the sleep of peace: Grant unto them, we beseech thee, thy mercy, and everlasting peace, and that, at the day of the general resurrection, we and all they which be of the mystical body of thy Son, may altogether be set on his right hand, and hear that his most joyful voice: Come unto me, O ye that be blessed of my Father, and possess the kingdom, which is prepared for you from the beginning of the world: grant this, O Father, for Jesus Christ's sake, our only Mediator and Advocate.

O God heavenly Father, which of thy tender mercy didst give thine only Son Jesu[z] Christ, to suffer death upon the cross for our redemption, who made there (by his one oblation, once offered) a full, perfect, and sufficient sacrifice, oblation, and satisfaction, for the sins of the whole world, and did institute, and in his holy Gospel command us to celebrate, a perpetual memory of that his precious death, until his coming again: Hear us (O merciful Father) we beseech thee; and with thy holy Spirit and word vouchsafe to bl✠ess and sanc✠tify these thy gifts, and creatures of bread and wine, that they may be unto us the body and blood of thy most dearly beloved Son Jesus Christ.

Here the Priest must take the bread into his hands. Who, in the same night that he was betrayed, took bread, and when he had blessed, and given thanks, he brake it, and gave it to his disciples, saying:

[z] In some copies, "Jesus."

Take, eat, this is my body which is given for you: do this in remembrance of me.

Likewise after supper he took the cup, and when he had given thanks, he gave it to them, saying: Drink ye all of this, for this is my blood of the new Testament, which is shed for you and for many, for remission of sins: Do this as oft as you shall drink it, in remembrance of me.

<small>Here the Priest shall take the cup into his hands.</small>

These words before rehearsed are to be said, turning still to the Altar, without any elevation, or shewing the Sacrament to the people.

WHEREFORE, O Lord and heavenly Father, according to the Institution of thy dearly beloved Son, our Saviour Jesu Christ, we thy humble servants do celebrate, and make here before thy divine Majesty, with these thy holy gifts, the memorial which thy Son hath willed us to make: having in remembrance his blessed passion, mighty resurrection, and glorious ascension, rendering unto thee most hearty thanks, for the innumerable benefits procured unto us by the same, entirely desiring thy fatherly goodness, mercifully to accept this our Sacrifice of praise and thanksgiving: most humbly beseeching thee to grant, that by the merits and death of thy Son Jesus Christ, and through faith in his blood, we and all thy whole church may obtain remission of our sins, and all other benefits of his passion. And here we offer and present unto thee (O Lord) ourself, our souls, and bodies, to be a reasonable, holy, and lively sacrifice unto thee: humbly beseeching thee, that whosoever shall be partakers[a] of this holy Communion, may worthily receive the most precious body and blood of thy Son Jesus Christ, and be fulfilled with thy grace and heavenly benediction, and made one body with thy Son Jesus

---

[a] In some copies, "partaker.

Christ, that he may dwell in them, and they in him. And although we be unworthy (through our manifold sins) to offer unto thee any Sacrifice : Yet we beseech thee to accept this our bounden duty and service, and command these our prayers and supplications, by the ministry of thy holy Angels, to be brought up into thy holy Tabernacle before the sight of thy divine Majesty ; not weighing our merits, but pardoning our offences, through Christ our Lord ; by whom, and with whom, in the unity of the Holy Ghost, all honour and glory be unto thee, O Father Almighty, world without end. Amen.

Let us pray.

As our Saviour Christ hath commanded and taught us, we are bold to say. Our Father, which art in heaven, hallowed be thy name. Thy Kingdom come. Thy will be done in earth, as it is in heaven. Give us this day our daily bread. And forgive us our trespasses, as we forgive them that trespass against us. And lead us not into temptation.

The Answer. But deliver us from evil. Amen [b].

Then shall the Priest say,

The peace of the Lord be alway with you.

The Clerks. And with thy spirit.

The Priest. Christ our paschal Lamb is offered up for us, once for all, when he bare our sins on his body upon the cross ; for he is the very Lamb of God, that taketh away the sins of the world : wherefore let us keep a joyful and holy feast with the Lord.

Here the Priest shall turn him toward those that come to the holy Communion, and shall say,

YOU that do truly and earnestly repent you of your sins to Almighty God, and be in love and charity with your neighbours, and intend to lead a new life, follow-

[b] In some copies, "Amen" *omitted.*

ing the commandments of God, and walking from henceforth in his holy ways: draw near and take this holy Sacrament to your comfort, make your humble confession to Almighty God, and to his holy church here gathered together in his name, meekly kneeling upon your knees.

Then shall this general Confession be made, in the name of all those that are minded to receive the holy Communion, either by one of them, or else by one of the ministers, or by the Priest himself, all kneeling humbly upon their knees.

ALMIGHTY GOD, Father of our Lord Jesus Christ, maker of all things, judge of all men, we knowledge and bewail our manifold sins and wickedness, which we from time to time, most grievously have committed, by thought, word and deed, against thy divine majesty, provoking most justly thy wrath and indignation against us: we do earnestly repent, and be heartily sorry for these our misdoings: the remembrance of them is grievous unto us, the burden of them is intolerable: have mercy upon us, have mercy upon us, most merciful Father, for thy Son our Lord Jesus Christ's sake, forgive us all that is past, and grant that we may ever hereafter serve and please thee in newness of life, to the honour and glory of thy name: Through Jesus Christ our Lord.

Then shall the Priest stand up, and turning himself to the people, say thus,

ALMIGHTY GOD, our heavenly Father, who of his great mercy, hath promised forgiveness of sins to all them, which with hearty repentance and true faith turn unto him: have mercy upon you, pardon and deliver you from all your sins, confirm and strengthen you in all goodness, and bring you to everlasting life: through Jesus Christ our Lord. Amen.

Then shall the Priest also say,

Hear what comfortable words our Saviour Christ saith, to all that truly turn to him.

Come unto me all that travail, and be heavy laden, and I shall refresh you. So God loved the world that he gave his only-begotten Son, to the end that all that believe in him, should not perish, but have life everlasting.

Hear also what Saint Paul sayeth.

This is a true saying, and worthy of all men to be received, that Jesus Christ came into this world to save sinners.

Hear also what Saint John sayeth.

If any man sin, we have an advocate with the Father, Jesus Christ the righteous, and he is the propitiation for our sins.

Then shall the Priest, turning him to God's board, kneel down, and say in the name of all them, that shall receive the Communion, this prayer following.

WE do not presume to come to this thy table (O merciful Lord) trusting in our own righteousness, but in thy manifold and great mercies: we be not worthy so much as to gather up the crumbs under thy table: but thou art the same Lord whose property is always to have mercy: Grant us therefore (gracious Lord) so to eat the flesh of thy dear Son Jesus [c] Christ, and to drink his blood in these holy Mysteries, that we may continually dwell in him, and he in us, that our sinful bodies may be made clean by his body, and our souls washed through his most precious blood. Amen.

¶ *Then shall the Priest first receive the Communion in both kinds himself, and next deliver it to other Ministers, if any be there present, (that they may be ready to help the chief Minister,) and after to the people.*

[c] In some copies, "Jesu."

¶ And when he delivereth the Sacrament of the body of Christ, he shall say to every one these words:

The body of our Lord Jesus Christ which was given for thee, preserve thy body and soul unto everlasting life.

And the Minister delivering the Sacrament of the blood, and giving every one to drink once and no more, shall say,

The blood of our Lord Jesus Christ which was shed for thee, preserve thy body and soul unto everlasting life.

If there be a Deacon or other Priest, then shall he follow with the Chalice: and as the Priest ministereth the Sacrament of the body, so shall he (for more expedition) minister the Sacrament of the blood, in form before written.

In the communion time the Clerks shall sing,

ii. O Lamb of God, that takest away the sins of the world : have mercy upon us.

O Lamb of God, that takest away the sins of the world : grant us thy peace.

Beginning so soon as the Priest doth receive the holy Communion, and when the Communion is ended, then shall the Clerks sing the post-Communion.

¶ Sentences of holy scripture, to be said or sung every day one, after the holy Communion, called the post-Communion.

IF any man will follow me, let him forsake himself, and take up his cross, and follow me. *Math.* xvi.

Whosoever shall endure unto the end, he shall be saved. *Mar.* xiii.

Praised be the Lord God of Israel, for he hath visited and redeemed his people : therefore let us serve him all the days of our life, in holiness and righteousness accepted before him. *Luc.* i.

Happy are those servants, whom the Lord (when he cometh) shall find waking. *Luc.* xii.

Be ye ready, for the Son of man will come at an hour when ye think not. *Luc.* xii.

The servant that knoweth his master's will, and hath not prepared himself, neither hath done according to his will, shall be beaten with many stripes. *Luc.* xii.

The hour cometh, and now it is, when true worshippers shall worship the Father in spirit and truth. *John* iv.

Behold, thou art made whole, sin no more, lest any worse thing happen unto thee. *John* v.

If ye shall continue in my word, then are ye my very disciples, and ye shall know the truth, and the truth shall make you free. *John* viii.

While ye have light, believe on the light, that ye may be the children of light. *John* xii.

He that hath my commandments, and keepeth them, the same is he that loveth me. *John* xiv.

If any man love me, he will keep my word, and my Father will love him, and we will come unto him, and dwell with him. *John* xiv.

If ye shall bide in me, and my word shall abide in you, ye shall ask what ye will, and it shall be done to you. *John* xv.

Herein is my Father glorified, that ye bear much fruit, and become my disciples. *John* xv.

This is my commandment, that you love together, as I have loved you. *John* xv.

If God be on our side, who can be against us? which did not spare his own Son, but gave him for us all. *Roma.* viii.

Who shall lay any thing to the charge of God's chosen? it is GOD that justifieth; who is [he] that can condemn? *Roma.* viii.

The night is past, and the day is at hand; let us therefore cast away the deeds of darkness, and put on the armour of light. *Rom.* xiii.

Christ Jesus is made of GOD, unto us, wisdom,

and righteousness, and sanctifying, and redemption, that (according as it is written) He which rejoiceth should rejoice in the Lord. 1 *Corin.* i.

Know ye not that ye are the temple of GOD, and that the Spirit of GOD dwelleth in you? If any man defile the temple of GOD, him shall God destroy. 1 *Corin.* iii.

Ye are dearly bought; therefore glorify God in your bodies, and in your spirits, for they belong to God. 1 *Cor.* vi.

Be you followers of God as dear children, and walk in love, even as Christ loved us, and gave himself for us an offering and a Sacrifice of a sweet savour to God. *Ephes.* v.

Then the Priest shall give thanks to God, in the name of all them that have communicated, turning him first to the people, and saying,

The Lord be with you.
The Answer. And with thy spirit.
The Priest. Let us pray.

ALMIGHTY and everliving [d] GOD, we most heartily thank thee, for that thou hast vouchsafed to feed us in these holy Mysteries, with the spiritual food of the most precious body and blood of thy Son our Saviour Jesus Christ, and hast assured us (duly receiving the same) of thy favour and goodness toward us, and that we be very members incorporate in thy mystical body, which is the blessed company of all faithful people, and heirs through hope of thy everlasting kingdom, by the merits of the most precious death and passion of thy dear Son. We therefore most humbly beseech thee, O heavenly Father, so to assist us with thy grace, that we may continue in that holy fellowship, and do all such good works, as thou hast prepared for us to walk in: through Jesus Christ our Lord, to whom,

---

[d] In some copies, "everlasting."

with thee and the Holy Ghost, be all honour and glory, world without end.

Then the Priest turning him to the people, shall let them depart with this blessing:

The peace of GOD (which passeth all understanding) keep your hearts and minds in the knowledge and love of GOD, and of his Son Jesus Christ our Lord : And the blessing of God Almighty, the Father, the Son, and the Holy Ghost, be amongst you and remain with you alway.

Then the people shall answer,

Amen.

Where there are no clerks, there the Priest shall say all things appointed here for them to sing.
When the holy Communion is celebrate on the workday, or in private houses: Then may be omitted, the Gloria in excelsis, the Creed, the Homily, and the exhortation, beginning,

DEARLY beloved, &c.

¶ *Collects to be said after the Offertory, when there is no Communion, every such day one.*

ASSIST us mercifully, O Lord, in these our supplications and prayers, and dispose the way of thy servants toward the attainment of everlasting salvation : that among all the changes and chances of this mortal life, they may ever be defended by thy most gracious and ready help ; through Christ our Lord. Amen.

O ALMIGHTY Lord and everliving GOD, vouchsafe, we beseech thee, to direct, sanctify, and govern, both our hearts and bodies, in the ways of thy laws, and in the works of thy commandments : that through thy most mighty protection, both here and ever, we may be preserved in body and soul : Through our Lord and Saviour Jesus Christ. Amen.

GRANT, we beseech thee, Almighty God, that the words which we have heard this day with our outward ears, may through thy grace be so grafted inwardly in our hearts, that they may bring forth in us the fruit of good living, to the honour and praise of thy name: through Jesus Christ our Lord. Amen.

PREVENT us, O Lord, in all our doings, with thy most gracious favour, and further us with thy continual help, that in all our works begun, continued, and ended in thee, we may glorify thy holy name, and finally by thy mercy obtain everlasting life: Through Jesus Christ our Lord. Amen [e].

ALMIGHTY God, the fountain of all wisdom, which knowest our necessities before we ask, and our ignorance in asking: we beseech thee to have compassion upon our infirmities, and those things, which for our unworthiness we dare not, and for our blindness we cannot ask, vouchsafe to give us for the worthiness of thy Son Jesu Christ our Lord. Amen.

ALMIGHTY God, which hast promised to hear the petitions of them that ask in thy Son's name, we beseech thee mercifully to incline thine ears to us that have made now our prayers and supplications unto thee: and grant that those things which we have faithfully asked according to thy will, may effectually be obtained to the relief of our necessity, and to the setting forth of thy glory: Through Jesus Christ our Lord.

¶ *For rain.*

O GOD heavenly Father, which by thy Son Jesu Christ hast promised to all them that seek thy kingdom, and the righteousness thereof, all things necessary to the bodily sustenance: send us, we beseech thee, in this our necessity, such moderate rain and showers, that we may receive the fruits of the earth,

---

[e] In some copies, "Through, &c."

to our comfort and to thy honour; Through Jesus Christ our Lord.

For fair weather.

O LORD God, which for the sin of man, didst once drown all the world, except eight persons, and afterward of thy great mercy, didst promise never to destroy it so again: We humbly beseech thee, that although we for our iniquities have worthily deserved this plague of rain and waters, yet, upon our true repentance, thou wilt send us such weather whereby we may receive the fruits of the earth in due season, and learn both by thy[f] punishment to amend our lives, and by the granting of our petition to give thee praise and glory: Through Jesu Christ our Lord.

¶ *Upon Wednesdays and Fridays, the English Litany shall be said or sung in all places, after such form as is appointed by the king's majesty's Injunctions: Or as is or shall be otherwise appointed by his highness*[g]. *And though there be none to communicate with the Priest, yet these days (after the Litany ended) the Priest shall put upon him a plain Albe or surplice, with a cope, and say all things at the Altar (appointed to be said at the celebration of the Lord's supper,) until after the offertory. And then shall add one or two of the Collects aforewritten, as occasion shall serve, by his discretion. And then turning him to the people shall let them depart with the accustomed blessing. And the same order shall be used all other days, whensoever the people be customably assembled to pray in the church, and none disposed to communicate with the Priest. Likewise in Chapels annexed, and all other places, there shall be no celebration of the Lord's supper, except there be some to commuicate with the Priest.*

And in such Chapels annexed where the people hath not been accustomed to pay any holy bread, there they must either

---

[f] In some copies, "thy" *omitted*.
[g] In some copies, the words "or as is or shall be otherwise appointed by his highness" are *omitted*.

make some charitable provision for the bearing of the charges of the Communion, or else (for receiving of the same) resort to their parish church.

For avoiding of all matters and occasion of dissension, it is meet that the bread prepared for the Communion be made, through all this realm, after one sort and fashion: that is to say, unleavened, and round, as it was afore, but without all [h] manner of print, and something more larger and thicker than it was, so that it may be aptly divided in divers pieces: and every one shall be divided in two pieces, at the least, or more, by the discretion of the minister, and so distributed. And men [i] must not think less to be received in part than in the whole, but in each of them the whole body of our Saviour Jesu Christ.

And forsomuch as the Pastors and Curates within this realm shall continually find at their costs and charges in their cures sufficient bread and wine for the holy Communion (as oft as their Parishioners shall be disposed for their spiritual comfort to receive the same) it is therefore ordered, that in recompence of such costs and charges, the Parishioners of every Parish shall offer every Sunday, at the time of the Offertory, the just valour and price of the holy loaf (with all such money and other things as were wont to be offered with the same) to the use of their Pastors and Curates, and that in such order and course, as they were wont to find and pay the said holy loaf.

Also that the receiving of the Sacrament of the blessed body and blood of Christ, may be most agreeable to the institution thereof, and to the usage of the primitive Church: In all [k] Cathedral and Collegiate churches, there shall always some communicate with the Priest that ministereth. And that the same may be also observed every where abroad in the country: Some one at the least of that house in every parish, to whom by course, after the ordinance herein made, it appertaineth to offer for the charges of the Communion, or some other whom they shall provide to offer for them, shall receive the holy Communion with the priest: the which may be the better done, for that they know before, when their

---

[h] In several copies, "any manner."   [i] In some copies, the word "men" omitted.   [k] In some copies, "all" omitted.

course cometh, and may therefore dispose themselves to the worthy receiving of the Sacrament. And with him or them who doth so offer the charges of the Communion, all other, who be then Godly disposed thereunto, shall likewise receive the Communion. And by this means the Minister having always some to communicate with him, may accordingly solemnise so high and holy mysteries, with all the suffrages and due order appointed for the same. And the Priest on the week day shall forbear to celebrate the Communion, except he have some that will communicate with him.

Furthermore, every man and woman to be bound to hear and be at the divine service, in the Parish church where they be resident, and there with devout prayer, or Godly silence and meditation, to occupy themselves. There to pay their duties, to communicate once in the year at the least, and there to receive and take all other Sacraments and rites, in this book appointed. And whosoever willingly, upon no just cause, doth absent themselves, or doth ungodly in the Parish church occupy themselves: upon proof thereof, by the Ecclesiastical laws of the Realm, to be excommunicate, or suffer other punishment, as shall to the Ecclesiastical judge (according to his discretion) seem convenient.

And although it be read in ancient writers, that the people, many years past, received at the Priest's hands the Sacrament of the body of Christ in their own hands, and no commandment of Christ to the contrary: Yet forasmuch as they many times conveyed the same secretly away, kept it with them, and diversely abused it to superstition and wickedness: lest any such thing hereafter should be attempted, and that an uniformity might be used throughout the whole realm, it is thought convenient the people commonly receive the Sacrament of Christ's body in their mouths, **at the Priest's hand.**

THE

LITANY AND SUFFRAGES[1].

O GOD the Father of heaven : have mercy upon us miserable sinners.

O God the Father of heaven : have mercy upon us miserable sinners [m].

O God the Son, Redeemer of the world : have mercy upon us miserable sinners.

O God the Son, Redeemer of the world : have mercy upon us miserable sinners.

O God the Holy Ghost, proceeding from the Father and the Son : have mercy upon us miserable sinners.

O God the Holy Ghost, proceeding from the Father and the Son : have mercy upon us miserable sinners.

O holy, blessed, and glorious Trinity, three Persons and one God : have mercy upon us miserable sinners.

O holy, blessed, and glorious Trinity, three persons and one God : have mercy upon us miserable sinners.

Remember not, Lord, our offences, nor the offences of our forefathers, neither take thou vengeance of our sins : spare us, good Lord, spare thy people, whom thou hast redeemed with thy most precious blood, and be not angry with us for ever.

Spare us, good Lord.

From all evil and mischief, from sin, from the crafts and assaults of the devil, from thy wrath, and from everlasting damnation :

Good Lord, deliver us.

---

[1] In the two earlier editions of the 1549 book, the Litany appears printed on a separate sheet, and added at the end. In the Prayer-Book of 1552, and afterwards, The Litany is printed immediately after the Order for Morning Prayer.

[m] In some copies, the words "miserable sinners" are *omitted* in the four responses, and "&c." put in their stead.

From blindness of heart, from pride, vainglory, and hypocrisy, from envy, hatred, and malice, and all uncharitableness :
Good Lord, deliver us.
From fornication, and all other[a] deadly sin, and from all the deceits of the world, the flesh, and the devil :
Good Lord, deliver us.
From lightning and tempest, from plague, pestilence, and famine, from battle and murther, and from sudden death :
Good Lord, deliver us.
From all sedition and privy conspiracy, from the tyranny of the Bishop of Rome and all his detestable enormities, from all false doctrine and heresy, from hardness of heart, and contempt of thy word and commandment :
Good Lord, deliver us.
By the mystery of thy holy incarnation, by thy holy nativity and Circumcision, by thy Baptism, fasting, and temptation :
Good Lord, deliver us.
By thine agony and bloody sweat, by thy cross and passion, by thy precious death and burial, by thy glorious resurrection and ascension, by the coming of the Holy Ghost :
Good Lord, deliver us.
In all time of our tribulation, in all time of our wealth, in the hour of death, in the day of judgment :
Good Lord, deliver us.
We sinners do beseech thee to hear us (O Lord God) and that it may please thee to rule and govern thy holy Church universal in the right way :
We beseech thee to hear us, good Lord.
That it may please thee to keep Edward the vi., thy servant our king and governor :
We beseech thee to hear us, good Lord.

[a] In some copies, the word "other" is *omitted.*

That it may please thee to rule his heart in thy faith, fear, and love, that he may always have affiance in thee, and ever seek thy honour and glory:
We beseech thee to hear us, good Lord.

That it may please thee to be his defender and keeper, giving him the victory over all his enemies:
We beseech thee to hear us, good Lord.

That it may please thee to illuminate all Bishops, pastors and ministers of the Church, with true knowledge and understanding of thy word, and that both by their preaching and living they may set it forth. and shew it accordingly:
We beseech thee to hear us, good Lord.

That it may please thee to endue the Lords of the council, and all the nobility, with grace, wisdom, and understanding:
We beseech thee to hear us, good Lord.

That it may please thee to bless and keep the magistrates, giving them grace to execute justice, and to maintain truth:
We beseech thee to hear us, good Lord.

That it may please thee to bless and keep all thy people:
We beseech thee to hear us, good Lord.

That it may please thee to give to all nations unity, peace, and concord:
We beseech thee to hear us, good Lord.

That it may please thee to give us an heart to love and dread thee, and diligently to live after thy commandments:
We beseech thee to hear us, good Lord.

That it may please thee to give all thy people increase of grace, to hear meekly thy word, and to receive it with pure affection, and to bring forth the fruits of the Spirit:
We beseech thee to hear us, good Lord.

That it may please thee to bring into the way of truth all such as have erred and are deceived :
We beseech thee to hear us, good Lord.

That it may please thee to strengthen such as do stand, and to comfort and help the weak-hearted, and to raise up them that fall, and finally to beat down Satan under our feet :
We beseech thee to hear us, good Lord.

That it may please thee to succour, help, and comfort all that be in danger, necessity, and tribulation :
We beseech thee to hear us, good Lord.

That it may please thee to preserve all that travel by land or by water, all women labouring of child, all sick persons, and young children, and to shew thy pity upon all prisoners and captives :
We beseech thee to hear us, good Lord.

That it may please thee to defend and provide for the fatherless children and widows, and all that be desolate and oppressed :
We beseech thee to hear us, good Lord.

That it may please thee to have mercy upon all men :
We beseech thee to hear us, good Lord.

That it may please thee to forgive our enemies, persecutors, and slanderers, and to turn their hearts :
We beseech thee to hear us, good Lord.

That it may please thee to give and preserve to our use the kindly fruits of the earth, so as in due time we may enjoy them :
We beseech thee to hear us, good Lord.

That it may please thee to give us true repentance ; to forgive us all our sins, negligences, and ignorances, and to endue us with the grace of thy holy Spirit to amend our lives according to thy holy word :
We beseech thee to hear us, good Lord.

Son of God : we beseech thee to hear us.
Son of God : we beseech thee to hear us.

O Lamb of God, that takest away the sins of the world :
Grant us thy peace.
O Lamb of God, that takest away the sins of the world :
Have mercy upon us.
O Christ, hear us.
O Christ, hear us.
Lord, have mercy upon us.
Lord, have mercy upon us.
Christ, have mercy upon us.
Christ, have mercy upon us.
Lord, have mercy upon us.
Lord, have mercy upon us.
Our Father, which art in heaven. *With the residue of the Paternoster.*
And lead us not into temptation.
But deliver us from evil°.
The Versicle. O Lord, deal not with us after our sins.
The Answer. Neither reward us after our iniquities.

Let us pray.

O GOD merciful Father, that despisest not the sighing of a contrite heart, nor the desire of such as be sorrowful, mercifully assist our prayers, that we make before thee in all our troubles and adversities, whensoever they oppress us : And graciously hear us, that those evils, which the craft and subtilty of the devil or man worketh against us, be brought to nought, and by the providence of thy goodness they may be dispersed, that we thy servants, being hurt by no persecutions, may evermore give thanks unto thee, in thy holy Church : through Jesu ᵖ Christ our Lord.

O Lord, arise, help us, and deliver us for thy name's sake.

° In some copies, "Amen" is *added.*   ᵖ In some copies, "Jesus."

O God, we have heard with our ears, and our fathers have declared unto us, the noble works that thou didst in their days, and in the old time before them.

O Lord, arise, help us, and deliver us, for thy honour.

Glory be to the Father, the Son, and to the Holy Ghost ⁹ : as it was in the beginning, is now, and ever shall be world without end. Amen.

From our enemies defend us, O Christ.
Graciously look upon our afflictions.

Pitifully behold the sorrows of our heart.
Mercifully forgive the sins of thy ʳ *people.*

Favourably with mercy hear our prayers.
O Son of David, have mercy upon us.

Both now and ever vouchsafe to hear us, Christ.
Graciously hear us, O Christ.
Graciously hear us, O Lord Christ.

The Versicle. O Lord, let thy mercy be shewed upon us.

The Answer. As we do put our trust in thee.

Let us pray.

WE humbly beseech thee, O Father, mercifully to look upon our infirmities, and for the glory of thy name's sake, turn from us all those evils that we most righteously have deserved ; and grant that in all our troubles we may put our whole trust and confidence in thy mercy, and evermore serve thee in pureness of living, to thy honour and glory : through our only mediator and advocate Jesus Christ our Lord. Amen.

⁹ In some copies, the doxology is printed as two verses.
ʳ In some copies, "the people."

ALMIGHTY God, which hast given us grace at this
time with one accord to make our common supplications unto thee, and dost promise, that
when two or three be gathered in thy
name, thou wilt grant their requests:
fulfil now, O Lord, the desires and
petitions of thy servants, as may
be most expedient for them,
granting us in this world
knowledge of thy truth, and
in the world to come,
life everlasting.
Amen.

OF THE

ADMINISTRATION OF PUBLIC BAPTISM
TO BE USED IN THE CHURCH.

It appeareth by ancient writers, that the Sacrament of Baptism in the old time was not commonly ministered but at two times in the year, at Easter and Whitsuntide, at which times it was openly ministered in the presence of all the congregation: Which custom (now being grown out of use) although it cannot for many considerations be well restored again, yet it is thought good to follow the same as near as conveniently may be: Wherefore the people are to be admonished, that it is most convenient that Baptism should not be ministered but upon Sundays and other holy days, when the most number of people may come together. As well for that the congregation there present may testify the receiving of them, that be newly baptized, into the number of Christ's Church, as also because in the Baptism of Infants, every man present may be put in remembrance of his own profession made to God in his Baptism. For which cause also, it is expedient that Baptism be ministered in the English tongue. Nevertheless (if necessity so require) children ought at all times to be baptized, either at the church or else at home.

PUBLIC BAPTISM.

When there are children to be baptized upon the Sunday or holy day, the parents shall give knowledge over night or in the morning, afore the beginning of Matins, to the curate. And then the Godfathers, Godmothers, and people, with the children, must be ready at the church door, either immediately afore the last Canticle at Matins, or else immediately afore the last Canticle at Evensong, as the Curate by his discretion shall appoint. And then, standing there, the Priest shall ask whether the children be baptized or no. If they answer, No, then shall the Priest say thus.

DEAR [a] beloved, forasmuch as all men be conceived and born in sin, and that no man born in sin can enter into the kingdom of God (except he be regenerate and born anew of water and the Holy Ghost;) I beseech you to call upon God the Father through our Lord Jesus Christ, that of his bounteous mercy he will grant to these children that thing which by nature they cannot have, that is to say, they may be baptized with the Holy Ghost, and received into Christ's holy church, and be made lively members of the same.

Then the Priest shall say,

Let us pray.

ALMIGHTY and everlasting God, which of thy justice didst destroy by floods of water the whole world for sin, except eight persons, whom of thy mercy (the same time) thou didst save in the Ark: And when thou didst drown in the Red Sea wicked King Pharao, with all his army, yet (at the same time) thou didst lead thy people the children of Israel safely through the midst thereof: whereby thou didst figure the washing of thy holy baptism: and by the baptism of thy wellbeloved Son Jesus Christ, thou didst sanctify the flood Jordan, and all other waters to this mystical washing away of sin: we beseech thee (for thy infinite mercies) that thou wilt mercifully look upon these children, and sanctify them with thy Holy Ghost, that by this wholesome laver of regeneration, whatsoever sin is in them, may be washed clean away; that they, being delivered from thy wrath, may be received into the ark of Christ's Church, and so saved from perishing: and being fervent in spirit, steadfast in faith, joyful through hope, rooted in charity, may ever serve thee: And finally attain to everlasting life, with all thy holy and chosen people. This grant

[a] In some copies, "Dearly."

us, we beseech thee, for Jesus Christ's sake our Lord. Amen.

¶ *Here shall the Priest ask what shall be the name of the child, and when the Godfathers and Godmothers have told the name, then he shall*[1] *make a cross upon the child's forehead and breast, saying,*

¶ *N.* Receive the sign of the holy Cross, both in thy forehead, and in thy breast, in token that thou shalt not be ashamed to confess thy faith in Christ crucified, and manfully to fight under his banner against sin, the world, and the devil, and to continue his faithful soldier and servant unto thy life's end. Amen.

And this he shall do and say to as many children as be present to be baptized, one after another.

Let us pray.

ALMIGHTY and immortal God, the aid of all that need, the helper of all that flee to thee for succour, the life of them that believe, and the resurrection of the dead: we call upon thee for these infants, that they coming to thy holy baptism, may receive remission of their sins, by spiritual regeneration. Receive them (O Lord) as thou hast promised by thy well beloved Son, saying: Ask, and you shall have: seek, and you shall find: knock, and it shall be opened unto you. So give now unto us that ask: let us that seek find: open thy gate upon us that knock: that these infants may enjoy the everlasting benediction of thy heavenly washing, and may come to the eternal kingdom which thou hast promised by Christ our Lord. Amen.

Then let the Priest looking upon the children, say,

I COMMAND thee, unclean spirit, in the name of the Father, of the Son, and of the Holy Ghost, that thou

---

[1] In some copies, "shall he."

come out, and depart from these infants, whom our Lord Jesus Christ hath vouchsafed to call to his holy Baptism, to be made members of his body, and of his holy congregation. Therefore, thou cursed spirit, remember thy sentence, remember thy judgment[u], remember the day to be at hand wherein thou shalt burn in fire everlasting, prepared for thee and thy Angels. And presume not hereafter to exercise any tyranny toward these infants, whom Christ hath bought with his precious blood, and by this his holy Baptism calleth[x] to be of his flock.

Then shall the Priest say,

The Lord be with you.
The People. And with thy spirit.
The Minister. ¶ Hear now the Gospel written by St. Mark.

At a certain time they brought children to Christ that he should touch them, and his disciples rebuked those that brought them. But when Jesus saw it, he was displeased, and said unto them: Suffer little children to come unto me, and forbid them not; (for to such belongeth the kingdom of God). Verily I say unto you: whosoever doth not receive the kingdom of God, as a little child, he shall not enter therein. And when he had taken them up in his arms, he put his hands upon them, and blessed them. *Mark x.*

After the Gospel is read, the Minister shall make this brief exhortation upon the words of the Gospel.

FRIENDS, you[y] hear in this Gospel the words of our Saviour Christ, that he commanded the children to be brought unto him: how he blamed those that would have kept them from him: how he exhorteth[z]

---

[u] In some copies, "judgements."   [x] In some copies, "called."
[y] In some copies, "ye."   [z] In some copies, "exhorted."

all men to follow their innocency. Ye perceive how by his outward gesture and deed he declared his good will toward them. For he embraced them in his arms, he laid his hands upon them, and blessed them. Doubt ye not therefore, but earnestly believe, that he will likewise favourably receive these present infants, that he will embrace them with the arms of his mercy, that he will give unto them the blessing of eternal life, and make them partakers of his everlasting kingdom. Wherefore we being thus persuaded of the good will of our heavenly Father toward these infants, declared by his Son Jesus Christ ; and nothing doubting but that he favourably alloweth this charitable work of ours, in bringing these children to his holy baptism: let us faithfully and devoutly give thanks unto him ; and say the prayer which the Lord himself taught. And in declaration of our faith, let us also recite the articles contained in our Creed.

Here the Minister, with the Godfathers [a]*, Godmothers, and people present, shall say,*

¶ Our Father, which art in heaven, hallowed be thy name, &c.

And then shall [b] *say openly.*

I believe in God the Father Almighty, &c.

The Priest shall add also this prayer,

ALMIGHTY and everlasting God, heavenly Father, we give thee humble thanks, that thou hast vouchsafed to call us to knowledge of thy grace, and faith in thee : increase and confirm this faith in us evermore : Give thy Holy Spirit to these infants, that they may be born again, and be made heirs of everlasting salvation, through our Lord Jesus Christ : who liveth

---

[a] In some copies, "Godfathers and." [b] In some copies, "shall he say."

and reigneth with thee and the Holy Spirit, now and for ever. Amen.

Then let the Priest take one of the children by the right hand, the other being brought after him. And coming into the church toward the font, say,

THE Lord vouchsafe to receive you into his holy household, and to keep and govern you alway in the same, that you may have everlasting life. Amen.

Then standing at the font the Priest shall speak to the Godfathers and Godmothers on this wise.

Wellbeloved friends, ye have brought these children here to be baptized; ye have prayed that our Lord Jesus Christ would vouchsafe to receive them, to lay his hands upon them, to bless them, to release them of their sins, to give them the kingdom of heaven, and everlasting life. Ye have heard also that our Lord Jesus Christ hath promised in his gospel, to grant all these things that ye have prayed for: which promise he for his part will most surely keep and perform. Wherefore, after this promise made by Christ, these infants must also faithfully for their part promise by you that be their sureties, that they will forsake the devil and all his works, and constantly believe God's holy word, and obediently keep his commandments.

Then shall the Priest demand of the child (which shall be first baptized) these questions following: first naming the child, and saying,

N. Dost thou forsake the devil and all his works?
Answer. I forsake them.
Minister. Dost thou forsake the vain pomp and glory of the world, with all the covetous desires of the same?
Answer. I forsake them.
Minister. Dost thou forsake the carnal desires of

the flesh, so that thou wilt not follow nor be led by them?

Answer. I forsake them.

Minister. Dost thou believe in God the Father Almighty, Maker of heaven and earth?

Answer. I believe.

Minister. Dost thou believe in Jesus Christ his only begotten Son our Lord, and that he was conceived by the Holy Ghost, born of the virgin Mary, that he suffered under Poncius Pilate, was crucified, dead, and buried; that he went down into hell, and also did rise again the third day; that he ascended into heaven, and sitteth on the right hand of God the Father Almighty: And from thence shall come again at the end of the world, to judge the quick and the dead: Dost thou believe this?

Answer. I believe.

Minister. Dost thou believe in the Holy Ghost, the holy Catholic Church, the Communion of Saints, Remission of Sins, Resurrection of the flesh and everlasting life after death?

Answer. I believe.

Minister. What dost thou desire?

Answer. Baptism.

Minister. Wilt thou be baptized?

Answer. I will.

¶ *Then the Priest shall take the child in his hands, and ask the name. And naming the child, shall dip it in the water thrice. First dipping the right side: Second, the left side: The third time [c] dipping the face toward the font: so it be discreetly and warily done, saying,*

¶ N. I baptize thee in the name of the Father, and of the Son, and of the Holy Ghost. Amen.

¶ *And if the child be weak, it shall suffice to pour water upon it, saying the foresaid words.* N. *I baptize thee, &c.*

[c] In some copies, "Third time."

Then the Godfathers and Godmothers shall take and lay their hands upon the child, and the minister shall put upon him his white vesture, commonly called the Chrisom; and say,

TAKE this white vesture for a token of the innocency, which by God's grace in this holy sacrament of baptism is given unto thee; and for a sign whereby thou art admonished, so long as thou livest, to give thyself to innocency of living, that, after this transitory life, thou mayest be partaker of the life everlasting. Amen.

Then the Priest shall anoint the infant upon the head, saying,

ALMIGHTY God, the Father of our Lord Jesus Christ, who hath regenerate thee by water and the Holy Ghost, and hath given unto thee remission of all thy sins: he vouchsafe to anoint thee with the unction of his Holy Spirit, and bring thee to the inheritance of everlasting life. Amen.

When there are many to be baptized, this order of demanding, baptizing, putting on the Chrisom, and anointing, shall be used severally with every child: those that be first baptized departing from the font, and remaining in some convenient place within the Church until all be baptized. At the last end, the Priest, calling the Godfathers and Godmothers together, shall say this short Exhortation following:

FORASMUCH as these children have promised by you to forsake the devil and all his works, to believe in God, and to serve him; you must remember, that it is your parts and duty to see that these infants be taught, so soon as they shall be able to learn, what a solemn vow, promise, and profession they have made by you. And that they may know these things the better, ye shall call upon them to hear sermons; and chiefly you shall provide that they may learn the Creed, the Lord's Prayer, and the Ten Commandments, in the English tongue, and all other things which a Christian man ought to know and believe to his soul's health: and that these children may be virtuously brought up to lead a godly and [d] Christian life; remembering always that baptism doth represent unto us our profession, which is, to follow the example of our Saviour Christ, and to be made like unto him; that as he died and rose again for us, so should we (which are baptized) die from sin, and rise again unto righteousness, continually mortifying all our evil and corrupt affections, and daily proceeding in all virtue and godliness of living.

¶ *The Minister shall command that the Chrisoms be brought to the church, and delivered to the Priests after the accustomed manner, at the purification of the mother of every child; And that the children be brought to the Bishop to be confirmed of him, so soon as they can say in their vulgar tongue the Articles of the Faith, the Lord's Prayer, and the Ten Commandments, and be further instructed in the Catechism, set forth for that purpose, accordingly as it is there expressed.*
And so let the congregation depart in the name of the Lord.

¶ *Note, that if the number of children to be baptized, and multitude of people present, be so great that they cannot conveniently stand at the church door; then let them stand within the church, in some convenient place, nigh unto the church door; and there all things be said and done, appointed to be said and done at the church door.*

[d] In some copies, "and a Christian."

OF THEM THAT BE
BAPTIZED IN PRIVATE HOUSES
IN TIME OF NECESSITY.

¶ *The Pastors and Curates shall oft admonish the people, that they defer not the baptism of infants any longer than the Sunday, or other holy day next after the child be born, unless upon a great and reasonable cause declared to the Curate and by him approved.*

And also they shall warn them, that without great cause, and necessity they baptize not children at home in their houses. And when great need shall compel them so to do, that then they minister it on this fashion.

¶ *First let them that be present call upon God for his grace, and say the Lord's prayer, if the time will suffer. And then one of them shall name the child, and dip him in the water, or pour water upon him, saying these words:*

¶ N. I baptize thee in the name of the Father, and of the Son, and of the Holy Ghost. Amen.

And let them not doubt, but that [e] *the child so baptized is lawfully and sufficiently baptized, and ought not to be baptized again, in the Church. But yet nevertheless, if the child which is after this sort baptized do afterward live, it is expedient that he* [f] *be brought into the Church, to the intent the Priest may examine and try whether the child be lawfully baptized or no. And if those that bring any child to the church do answer that he is already baptized: Then shall the Priest examine them further.*

¶ By whom the child was baptized?
Who was present when the child was baptized?
Whether they called upon God for grace and succour in that necessity?
With what thing, or what matter, they did baptize the child?
With what words the child was baptized?

[e] In some copies, "but the child."   [f] In some copies, "they be."

Whether they think the child to be lawfully and perfectly baptized?

And if the minister[g] shall prove by the answers of such as brought the child, that all things were done, as they ought to be: Then shall not he christen the child again, but shall receive him, as one of the flock of the [b] true christian people, saying thus.

I CERTIFY you, that in this case ye have done well, and according unto due order concerning the baptizing of this child, which being born in original sin, and in the wrath of God, is now by the laver of regeneration in Baptism made the child of God, and heir of everlasting life: for our Lord Jesus Christ doth not deny his grace and mercy unto such infants, but most lovingly doth call them unto him: as the holy gospel doth witness to our comfort on this wise.

AT a certain time they brought children unto Christ that he should touch them, and his disciples rebuked those that brought them. But when Jesus saw it, he was displeased, and said unto them: Suffer little children to come unto me, and forbid them not, for to such belongeth the kingdom of God. Verily I say unto you, whosoever doth not receive the kingdom of God as a little child, he shall not enter therein. And when he had taken them up in his arms, he put his hands upon them and blessed them. *Mark x.*

After the Gospel is read: the minister shall make this exhortation upon the words of the gospel.

FRIENDS, ye hear in this gospel the words of our Saviour Christ, that he commanded the children to be brought unto him, how he blamed those that would have kept them from him, how he exhorted all men to follow their innocency: ye perceive how by his outward gesture and deed he declared his good will toward them; for he embraced them in his arms, he laid his hands upon them, and blessed them.

[g] In some copies, "ministers."   [h] In some copies, "of true."

Doubt you not therefore, but earnestly believe, that he hath likewise favourably received this present infant, that he hath embraced him with the arms of his mercy, that he hath given unto him the blessing of eternal life, and made him partaker of his everlasting kingdom. Wherefore we being thus persuaded of the good will of our heavenly Father, declared by his Son Jesus Christ towards this infant: Let us faithfully and devoutly give thanks unto him, and say the prayer which the Lord himself taught; and in declaration of our faith, let us also recite the articles contained in our Creed.

Here the minister with the Godfathers and Godmothers shall say.

OUR Father which art in heaven, hallowed be thy name: let Thy kingdom come, &c.[i]

Then shall they say the Creed, and then the Priest shall demand the name of the child, which being by the Godfathers and Godmothers pronounced, the minister shall say,

¶ *N.* Dost thou forsake the devil and all his works?

Answer. I forsake them.

Minister. Dost thou forsake the vain pomp and glory of the world, with all the covetous desires of the same?

Answer. I forsake them.

Minister. Dost thou forsake the carnal desires of the flesh, so that thou wilt not follow and[j] be led by them?

Answer. I forsake them.

Minister. Dost thou believe in God the Father almighty, maker of heaven and earth?

Answer. I believe.

Minister. Dost thou believe in Jesus Christ his

---

[i] In some copies, "hallowed be thy name, &c."
[j] In some copies, "nor."

only-begotten Son our Lord, and that he was conceived by the Holy Ghost, born of the virgin Mary, that he suffered under Pontius Pilate, was crucified, dead, and buried, that he went down into hell, and also did arise[k] again the third day, that he ascended into heaven, and sitteth on the right hand of God the Father almighty, and from thence shall come again at the end of the world to judge the quick and the dead: dost thou believe thus?

Answer. I believe.

Minister. Dost thou believe in the Holy Ghost, the holy catholic Church, the Communion of Saints, Remission of sins, Resurrection of the flesh, and everlasting life after death?

Answer. I believe.

Then the minister shall put the white vesture, commonly called the Chrisom, upon the child, saying,

TAKE this white vesture for a token of the innocency, which by God's grace in the[l] holy sacrament of Baptism is given unto thee, and for a sign whereby thou art admonished so long as thou shalt live[m], to give thyself to innocency of living, that after this transitory life thou mayest be partaker of the life everlasting. Amen.

¶ Let us pray.

ALMIGHTY and everlasting God, heavenly Father, we give thee humble thanks that thou hast vouchsafed to call us to the knowledge of thy grace, and faith in thee: Increase and confirm this faith in us evermore: Give thy Holy Spirit to this infant, that he being born again, and being made heir of everlasting salvation through our Lord Jesus Christ, may continue thy servant, and attain thy promises[n],

---

[k] In some copies, "rise."
[m] In some copies, "thou livest."
[l] In some copies, "this."
[n] In some copies, "promise."

through the same our Lord Jesus Christ thy Son: who liveth and reigneth with thee in unity of the same Holy Spirit everlastingly. Amen.

Then shall the minister make this exhortation to the Godfathers and Godmothers.

FORASMUCH as this child hath promised by you to forsake the devil and all his works, to believe in God, and to serve him, you must remember that it is your parts and duty to see that this infant be taught, so soon as he shall be able to learn, what a solemn vow, promise, and profession he hath made by you: and that he may know these things the better, ye shall call upon him to hear sermons: and chiefly ye shall provide that he may learn the Creed, the Lord's prayer, and the ten commandments in the English tongue, and all other things which a christian man ought to know and believe to his soul's health, and that this child may be virtuously brought up to lead a godly and a christian life: remembering alway that Baptism doth represent unto us our profession, which is to follow the example of our Saviour Christ, and to be made like unto him, that as he died and rose again for us, so should we, which are baptized, die from sin, and rise again unto righteousness, continually mortifying all our evil and corrupt affections, and daily proceeding in all virtue and godliness of living.

&c. As in Public Baptism.

¶ *But if they which bring the infants to the church, do make an uncertain answer to the priest's questions, and say that they cannot tell what they thought, did, or said, in that great fear and trouble of mind (as oftentimes it chanceth): Then let the Priest baptize him in form above written, concerning public Baptism, saving that at the dipping of the child in the font he shall use this form of words.*

IF thou be not baptized already, N. I baptize thee

in the name of the Father, and of the Son, and of the Holy Ghost. Amen.

The water in the font shall be changed every month once at the least, and afore any child be baptized in the water so changed, the Priest shall say at the font these prayers following.

O MOST merciful God our Saviour Jesu Christ, who hast ordained the element of water for the regeneration of thy faithful people, upon whom, being baptized in the river of Jordan, the Holy Ghost came down in º likeness of a dove: Send down, we beseech thee, the same thy Holy Spirit to assist us, and to be present at this our invocation of thy holy name: Sanctify ✠ this fountain of baptism, thou that art the sanctifier of all things, that by the power of thy word all those that shall be baptized therein may be spiritually regenerated, and made the children of everlasting adoption. Amen.

O MERCIFUL God, grant that the old Adam, in them that shall be baptized in this fountain, may be so ᵖ buried, that the new man may be raised up again. Amen.

GRANT that all carnal affections may die in them; and that all things, belonging to the Spirit, may live and grow in them. Amen.

GRANT to all them which at this fountain forsake the devil and all his works: that they may have power and strength to have victory and to triumph against him, the world, and the flesh. Amen.

WHOSOEVER shall confess thee, O Lord: recognise him also in thy kingdom. Amen.

GRANT that all sin and vice here may be so extinct: that they never have power to reign in thy servants. Amen.

º In some copies, "in the likeness."   ᵖ In some copies, "may so be."

GRANT that whosoever here shall begin to be of thy flock: may evermore continue in the same. Amen.

GRANT that all they which for thy sake in this life do deny and forsake themselves: may win and purchase thee, O Lord, which art everlasting treasure. Amen.

GRANT that whosoever is here dedicated to thee by our office and ministry: may also be endued with heavenly virtues, and everlastingly rewarded through thy mercy, O blessed Lord God, who dost live and govern all things world without end. Amen.

> The Lord be with you.
> *Answer.* And with thy spirit.

ALMIGHTY everliving [q] God, whose most dearly beloved Son Jesus Christ for the forgiveness of our sins did shed out of his most precious side both water and blood, and gave commandment to his disciples that they should go [r] teach all nations, and baptize them in the name of the Father, the Son, and the Holy Ghost: Regard, we beseech thee, the supplications of thy congregation, and grant that all thy servants which shall be baptized in this water, prepared for the ministration of thy holy sacrament, may receive the fulness of thy grace, and ever remain in the number of thy faithful and elect children, through Jesus Christ our Lord.

[q] In some copies, "everlasting."   [r] In some copies, "go and teach."

CONFIRMATION,
WHEREIN IS CONTAINED A CATECHISM FOR CHILDREN.

To the end that confirmation may be ministered to the more edifying of such as shall receive it (according to St. Paul's doctrine, who teacheth that all things should be done in the church to the edification of the same) it is thought good that none hereafter shall be confirmed, but such as can say in their mother tongue the articles of the faith, the Lord's prayer, and the ten commandments; and can also answer to such questions of this short Catechism, as the Bishop (or such as he shall appoint) shall by his discretion appose them in. And this order is most convenient to be observed for divers considerations.

¶ *First, because that when children come to the years of discretion, and have learned what their Godfathers and Godmothers promised for them in Baptism, they may then themselves with their own mouth, and with their own consent, openly before the church, ratify and confess the same, and also promise that by the grace of God they will evermore endeavour themselves faithfully to observe and keep such things, as they by their own mouth and confession have assented unto.*

¶ *Secondly, forasmuch as confirmation is ministered to them that be baptized, that by imposition of hands and prayer they may receive strength and defence against all temptations to sin, and the assault of the world, and the devil: it is most meet to be ministered, when children come to that age, that partly by the frailty of their own flesh, partly by the assaults of the world and the devil, they begin to be in danger to fall into sin.*

¶ *Thirdly, for that it is agreeable with the usage of the church in times past, whereby*[a] *it was ordained, that Confirmation should be ministered to them that were of perfect age, that they being instructed in Christ's religion, should openly profess their own faith, and promise to be obedient unto the will of God.*

[a] In some copies, "where."

¶ *And that no man shall think that any detriment shall come to children by deferring of their confirmation: he shall know for truth, that it is certain by God's word, that children being baptized (if they depart out of this life in their infancy) are undoubtedly saved.*

A CATECHISM,

THAT IS TO SAY,

AN INSTRUCTION TO BE LEARNED OF EVERY CHILD, BEFORE HE BE BROUGHT TO BE CONFIRMED OF THE BISHOP.

Question. WHAT is your name?
Answer. N or M.
Question. Who gave you this name?
Answer. My Godfathers and Godmothers in my Baptism, wherein I was made a member of Christ, the child of God, and an [1] inheritor of the kingdom of heaven.
Question. What did your Godfathers and Godmothers then for you?
Answer. They did promise and vow three things in my name. First, that I should forsake the devil and all his works and pomps, the vanities of the wicked world, and all the sinful lusts of the flesh. Secondly, that I should believe all the articles of the Christian faith. And thirdly, that I should keep God's holy will and commandments, and walk in the same all the days of my life.
Question. Dost thou not think that thou art bound to believe, and to do as they have promised for thee?
Answer. Yes verily. And by God's help so I will. And I heartily thank our heavenly Father, that he hath called me to this state of salvation, through Jesus

---

[1] In some copies, "and inheritor."

Christ our Saviour. And I pray God to give me his [u] grace, that I may continue in the same unto my life's end.

Question. Rehearse the articles of thy belief.

Answer. I believe in God the Father Almighty, maker of heaven and earth. And in Jesus Christ his only Son our Lord. Which was conceived by the Holy Ghost, born of the virgin Mary. Suffered under Ponce Pilate, was crucified, dead, and buried, he descended into hell. The third day he rose again from the dead. He ascended into heaven, and sitteth on the right hand of God the Father almighty. From thence shall he come to judge the quick and the dead. I believe in the Holy Ghost. The holy catholic church. The communion of saints. The forgiveness of sins. The resurrection of the body. And the life everlasting. Amen.

Question. What dost thou chiefly learn in these articles of thy belief?

Answer. First, I learn to believe in God the Father, who hath made me and all the world.

Secondly, in God the Son, who hath redeemed me and all mankind.

Thirdly, in God the Holy Ghost, who sanctifieth me and all the elect people of God.

Question. You said that your Godfathers and Godmothers did promise for you that ye should keep God's commandments. Tell me how many there be.

Answer. Ten.

Question. Which be they?

Answer. Thou shalt have none other Gods but me.

II. Thou shalt not make to thyself any graven image, nor the likeness of any thing that is in heaven above, or in the earth beneath, nor in the water under the earth: thou shalt not bow down to them, nor worship them.

III. Thou shalt not take the name of the Lord thy God in vain.

---

[u] In some copies, "the."

IV. Remember that thou keep holy the Sabbath day.
V. Honour thy father and thy mother.
VI. Thou shalt do no murder.
VII. Thou shalt not commit adultery.
VIII. Thou shalt not steal.
IX. Thou shalt not bear false witness against thy neighbour.
X. Thou shalt not covet thy neighbour's wife, nor his servant, nor his maid, nor his ox, nor his ass, nor any thing that is his.

Question. What dost thou chiefly learn by these commandments?

Answer. I learn two things: my duty towards God, and my duty towards my neighbour.

Question. What is thy duty towards God?

Answer. My duty towards God is, to believe in him. To fear him. And to love him with all my heart, with all my mind, with all my soul, and [v] with all my strength. To worship him. To give him thanks. To put my whole trust in him. To call upon him. To honour his holy name and his word, and to serve him truly all the days of my life.

Question. What is thy duty towards thy neighbour?

Answer. My duty towards my neighbour is, to love him as myself. And to do to all men as I would they should do to me. To love, honour, and succour my father and mother. To honour and obey the king and his ministers. To submit myself to all my governors, teachers, spiritual pastors, and masters. To order myself lowly and reverently to all my betters. To hurt no body by word nor deed. To be true and just in all my dealing. To bear no malice nor hatred in my heart. To keep my hands from picking and stealing, and my tongue from evil speaking, lying, and slandering. To keep my body in temperance, soberness, and chastity. Not to covet nor desire other men's goods. But learn and labour truly to

---

[v] In some copies, "and" *omitted*.

get my own living, and to do my duty in that state of life, unto which it shall please God to call me.

Question. My good son, know this, that thou art not able to do these things of thyself, nor to walk in the commandments of God and to serve him, without his special grace, which thou must learn at all times to call for by diligent prayer. Let me hear therefore if thou canst say the Lord's prayer.

Answer. Our Father which art in heaven, hallowed be thy name. Thy kingdom come. Thy will be done in earth as it is in heaven. Give us this day our daily bread. And forgive us our trespasses, as we forgive them that trespass against us. And lead us not into temptation, but deliver us from evil. Amen.

Question. What desirest thou of God in this prayer?
Answer. I desire my Lord God our heavenly Father, who is the giver of all goodness, to send his grace unto me, and to all people, that we may worship him, serve him, and obey him, as we ought to do. And I pray unto God, that he will send us all things that be needful both for our souls and bodies: And that he will be merciful unto us, and forgive us our sins: And that it will please him to save and defend us in all dangers ghostly and bodily: And that he will keep us from all sin and wickedness, and from our ghostly enemy, and from everlasting death. And this I trust he will do of his mercy and goodness, through our Lord Jesu Christ. And therefore I say, Amen. So be it.

¶ *So soon as the children can say in their mother tongue the articles of the faith, the Lord's prayer, the ten commandments, and also can answer to such questions of this short Catechism as the Bishop (or such as he shall appoint) shall by his discretion appose them in: then shall they be brought to the Bishop by one that shall be his Godfather or Godmother, that every child may have a witness of his Confirmation.*

¶ *And the Bishop shall confirm them on this wise.*

¶ CONFIRMATION.

Our help is in the name of the Lord.
Answer. Which hath made both heaven and earth.
Minister. Blessed is the name of the Lord.
Answer. Henceforth world without end.
Minister. The Lord be with you.
Answer. And with thy spirit.

Let us pray.

ALMIGHTY and everliving God, who hast vouchsafed to regenerate these thy servants of water and the Holy Ghost: And hast given unto them forgiveness of all their sins: Send down from heaven, we beseech thee, O Lord, upon them thy Holy Ghost the Comforter, with the manifold gifts of grace, the spirit of wisdom and understanding; the spirit of counsel and ghostly strength; the spirit of knowledge and true godliness, and fulfil them, O Lord, with the spirit of thy holy fear.

Answer. Amen.

Minister. Sign them, O Lord, and mark them to be thine for ever, by the virtue of thy holy cross and passion. Confirm and strength them with the inward unction of thy Holy Ghost, mercifully unto everlasting life. Amen.

Then the Bishop shall cross them in the forehead, and lay his hand upon their head[1], saying,

N. I sign thee with the sign of the cross, and lay my hand upon thee: In the name of the Father, and of the Son, and of the Holy Ghost. Amen.

And thus shall he do to every child one after another. And when he hath laid his hand upon every child, then shall he say.

The peace of the Lord abide with you.
Answer. And with thy spirit.

---

[1] In some copies, "heads."

CONFIRMATION.

Then shall the Bishop say [7].

¶ Let us pray.

ALMIGHTY everliving [2] God, which makest us both to will and to do those things that be good and acceptable unto thy majesty: we make our humble supplications unto thee for these children, upon whom (after the example of thy holy apostles) we have laid our hands, to certify them (by this sign) of thy favour and gracious goodness toward them: let thy fatherly hand (we beseech thee) ever be over them, let thy Holy Spirit ever be with them, and so lead them in the knowledge and obedience of thy word, that in the end they may obtain the life everlasting, through our Lord Jesus Christ, who with thee and the Holy Ghost liveth and reigneth one God world without end. Amen.

Then shall the Bishop bless the children, thus saying.

The blessing of God Almighty, the Father, the Son, and the Holy Ghost, be upon you, and remain with you for ever. Amen.

The Curate of every parish once in six weeks at the least, upon warning by him given, shall upon some Sunday or holy day, half an hour before evensong, openly in the church instruct and examine so many children of his parish sent unto him, as the time will serve, and as he shall think convenient, in some part of this Catechism. And all fathers, mothers, masters, and dames, shall cause their children, servants, and prentices (which are not yet confirmed), to come to the church at the day appointed, and obediently hear and be ordered by the Curate, until such time as they have learned all that is here appointed for them to learn.

¶ *And whensoever the Bishop shall give knowledge for children to be brought afore him to any convenient place, for their confirmation: Then shall the Curate of every parish*

---

[7] In some copies, rubrick *omitted*.   [2] In some copies, "everlasting."

either bring, or send in writing, the names of all those children of his parish which can say the articles of their faith, the Lord's prayer, and the ten commandments. And also how many of them can answer to the other questions contained in this Catechism.

¶ *And there shall none be admitted to the holy communion, until such time as he be confirmed.*

THE FORM OF
SOLEMNIZATION OF MATRIMONY.

¶ *First the banns must be asked three several Sundays or holy days, in the service time, the people being present, after the accustomed manner.*

And if the persons that would be married dwell in divers parishes, the banns must be asked in both parishes, and the Curate of the one parish shall not solemnize matrimony betwixt them, without a certificate of the banns being thrice asked, from the Curate of the other parish.

At the day appointed for Solemnization of Matrimony, the persons to be married shall come into the body of the Church, with their friends and neighbours. And there the priest shall thus say.

DEARLY beloved friends, we are gathered together here in the sight of God, and in the face of his congregation, to join together this man and this woman in holy matrimony, which is an honourable estate, instituted of God in paradise, in the time of man's innocency, signifying unto us the mystical union that is betwixt Christ and his church: which holy estate Christ adorned and beautified with his presence, and first miracle that he wrought, in Cana of Galilee, and is commended of Saint Paul to be honourable among all men ; and therefore is not to be enterprised, nor taken in hand unadvisedly, lightly, or wantonly, to satisfy men's carnal lusts and appetites, like brute beasts that have no understanding: but reverently, discreetly, advisedly, soberly, and in the fear of God : duly considering the causes for the which matrimony was ordained. One cause was the procreation of children, to be brought up in the fear and nurture of the Lord, and praise of God. Secondly it was ordained for a remedy against sin, and to avoid fornication, that such persons as be married, might live chastely in matrimony, and keep themselves undefiled members of Christ's body. Thirdly for the mutual society, help, and comfort, that the one ought to have of the other, both in prosperity and adversity. Into the which holy estate these two persons present come now to be joined. Therefore if any man can shew any just cause why they may not lawfully be joined so together: Let him now speak, or else hereafter for ever hold his peace.

And also speaking to the persons that shall be married, he shall say.

I REQUIRE and charge you (as you will answer at the dreadful day of judgment, when the secrets of all hearts shall be disclosed) that if either of you do know any impediment, why ye may not be lawfully joined together in matrimony, that ye confess it. For be ye well assured, that so many as be coupled together otherwise than God's word doth allow, are not joined of God, neither is their matrimony lawful.

At which day of marriage if any man do allege any impediment why they may not be coupled together in matrimony; and will be bound, and sureties with him, to the parties, or else put in a caution to the full value of such charges as the persons to be married do sustain, to prove his allegation: then the Solemnization must be deferred, unto such time as the truth be tried. If no impediment be alleged, then shall the Curate say unto the man.

N. WILT thou have this woman to thy wedded wife, to live together after God's ordinance in the holy estate of matrimony? Wilt thou love her, comfort her, honour, and keep her in sickness and in health? and forsaking all other keep thee only to her, so long as you both shall live?

The man shall answer,

I will.

Then shall the Priest say to* the woman.

N. Wilt thou have this man to thy wedded husband, to live together after God's ordinance, in the holy estate of matrimony? Wilt thou obey him, and serve him, love, honour, and keep him in sickness and in health? and forsaking all other keep thee only to him, so long as you both shall live?

The woman shall answer,
I will.

Then shall the Minister say,
Who giveth this woman to be married to this man?

And the minister receiving the woman at her father or friend's hands, shall cause the man to take the woman by the right hand, and so either to give their troth to other: The man first saying,

I *N.* take thee *N.* to my wedded wife, to have and to hold from this day forward, for better, for worse, for richer, for poorer, in sickness, and in health, to love, and to cherish, till death us depart: according to God's holy ordinance: And thereto I plight thee my troth.

Then shall they loose their hands, and the woman taking again the man by the right hand shall say,

I *N.* take thee *N.* to my wedded husband, to have and to hold from this day forward, for better, for worse, for richer, for poorer, in sickness, and in health, to love, cherish, and to obey, till death us depart: according to God's holy ordinance: And thereto I give thee my troth.

Then shall they again loose their hands, and the man shall give unto the woman a ring, and other tokens of spousage, as gold or silver, laying the same upon the book. And the Priest taking the ring shall deliver it unto the man, to put

* In some copies, "unto."

it upon the fourth finger of the woman's left hand. And the man taught by the priest, shall say,

¶ With this ring I thee wed : This gold and silver I thee give : with my body I thee worship : and with all my worldly goods I thee endow : In the name of the Father, and of the Son, and of the Holy Ghost. Amen.

Then the man leaving the ring upon the fourth finger of the woman's left hand, the minister shall say,

¶ Let us pray.

O ETERNAL God, creator and preserver of all mankind, giver of all spiritual grace, the author of everlasting life : send thy blessing upon these thy servants, this man and this woman, whom we bless in thy name, that as Isaac and Rebecca (after bracelets and jewels of gold given of the one to the other for tokens of their matrimony) lived faithfully together ; so these persons may surely perform and keep the vow and covenant betwixt them made, whereof this ring given and received is a token and pledge : and may ever remain in perfect love and peace together ; and live according to thy laws ; through Jesus Christ our Lord. Amen.

Then shall the Priest join their right hands together, and say,

¶ Those whom God hath joined together, let no man put asunder.

Then shall the minister speak unto the people.

FORASMUCH as *N.* and *N.* have consented together in holy wedlock, and have witnessed the same here before God and this company; and thereto have given and pledged their troth either to other, and have declared the same by giving and receiving gold and silver, and by joining of hands : I pronounce that they be man and wife together : In the name of the Father, of the Son, and of the Holy Ghost. Amen.

And the minister shall add this blessing.

¶ God the Father bless you. ✠ God the Son keep you: God the Holy Ghost lighten your understanding: The Lord mercifully with his favour look upon you, and so fill you with all spiritual benediction, and grace, that you may have remission of your sins in this life, and in the world to come life everlasting. Amen.

Then shall they go into the quire, and the ministers or clerk shall say or sing this Psalm following.

BLESSED are all they that fear the Lord, and walk in his ways. *Beati omnes. cxxviii.*

For thou shalt eat the labour of thy hands. O well is thee, and happy shalt thou be.

Thy wife shall be as the fruitful vine, upon the walls of thy house.

Thy children like the olive branches round about thy table.

Lo, thus shall the man be blessed, that feareth the Lord.

The Lord from out of Sion shall bless thee: that thou shalt see Hierusalem in prosperity all thy life long.

Yea, that thou shalt see thy children's children: and peace upon Israel.

Glory to the Father, &c.

As it was in the beginning, &c.

Or else this Psalm following.

GOD be merciful unto us, and bless us, and shew us the light of his countenance: and be merciful unto us. *Deus misereatur nostri. Psalm lxvii.*

That thy way may be known upon the earth, thy saving health among all nations.

Let the people praise thee (O God) yea, let all people praise thee.

O let the nations rejoice and be glad, for thou shalt judge the flock righteously, and govern the nations upon the earth.

Let the people praise thee (O God) let all the people praise thee.

Then shall the earth bring forth her increase: and God, even our own God, shall give us his blessing.

God shall bless us, and all the ends of the world shall fear him.

Glory to the Father, &c.

As it was in the, &c.

The Psalm ended, and the man and woman kneeling afore the altar, the priest standing at the altar, and turning his face toward them, shall say,

Lord, have mercy upon us.

Answer. Christ, have mercy upon us.

Minister. Lord, have mercy upon us.

¶ Our Father which art in heaven, &c.

And lead us not into temptation.

Answer. But deliver us from evil.   Amen.

Minister. O Lord, save thy servant, and thy handmaid.

Answer. Which put their trust in thee.

Minister. O Lord, send them help from thy holy place.

Answer. And evermore defend them.

Minister. Be unto them a tower of strength [b].

Answer. From the face of their enemy.

Minister. O Lord, hear my prayer.

Answer. And let my cry come unto thee.

The Minister. Let us pray.

O GOD of Abraham, God of Isaac, God of Jacob, bless these thy servants, and sow the seed of eternal life in their minds, that whatsoever in thy holy word they shall profitably learn, they may in deed fulfil the same. Look, O Lord, mercifully upon them from

---

[b] In some copies, "a tower of defence."

heaven, and bless them : And as thou didst send thy Angel Raphael to Thobie and Sara, the daughter of Raguel, to their great comfort ; so vouchsafe to send thy blessing upon these thy servants, that they obeying thy will, and alway being in safety under thy protection, may abide in thy love unto their lives' end : through Jesu Christ our Lord. Amen.

This prayer following shall be omitted where the woman is past child-birth.

O MERCIFUL Lord, and heavenly Father, by whose gracious gift mankind is increased : We beseech thee, assist with thy blessing these two persons, that they may both be fruitful in procreation of children ; and also live together so long in godly love and honesty, that they may see their childer's children unto the third and fourth generation, unto thy [c] praise and honour : through Jesus Christ our Lord. Amen.

O God, which by thy mighty power hast made all things of nought, which also after other things set in order didst appoint that out of man (created after thine own image and similitude) woman should take her beginning : and, knitting them together, didst teach, that it should never be lawful to put asunder those, whom thou by matrimony hadst made one : O God, which hast consecrated the state of matrimony to such an excellent mystery, that in it is signified and represented the spiritual marriage and unity betwixt Christ and his church : Look mercifully upon these thy servants, that both this man may love his wife, according to thy word, (as Christ did love his spouse the church, who gave himself for it, loving and cherishing it even as his own flesh ;) and also that this woman may be loving and amiable to her husband as Rachael, wise as Rebecca, faithful and obedient as Sara ; and in all quietness, sobriety, and peace, be a follower of holy and godly matrons. O Lord, bless

[c] In some copies, "the."

them both, and grant them to inherit thy [d] everlasting kingdom, through Jesus [e] Christ our Lord. Amen.

Then shall the Priest bless the man and the woman, saying,

ALMIGHTY God, which at the beginning did create our first parents Adam and Eve, and did sanctify and join them together in marriage: Pour upon you the riches of his grace, sanctify and ✠ bless you, that ye may please him both in body and soul, and live together in holy love unto your lives' end. Amen.

Then shall be said after the gospel a sermon, wherein ordinarily (so oft as there is any marriage) the office of man and wife shall be declared according to holy scripture. Or if there be no sermon, the minister shall read this that followeth.

ALL ye which be married, or which intend to take the holy estate of matrimony upon you: hear what holy scripture doth say, as touching the duty of husbands toward their wives, and wives toward their husbands.

Saint Paul (in his Epistle to the Ephesians the fifth chapter) doth give this commandment to all married men.

Ye husbands, love your wives, even as Christ loved the church, and hath given himself for it, to sanctify it, purging it in the fountain of water, through the word, that he might make it unto himself a glorious congregation, not having spot, or wrinkle, or any such thing; but that it should be holy and blameless. So men are bound to love their own wives as their own bodies: he that loveth his own wife, loveth himself. For never did any man hate his own flesh, but nourisheth and cherisheth it, even as the Lord doth the congregation; for we are members of his body, of his flesh, and of his bones. For this cause shall a man leave father and mother, and shall be joined unto his wife, and they two shall be one flesh. This

---

[d] In some copies, "the."   [e] In some copies, "Jesu."

mystery is great, but I speak of Christ and of the congregation. Nevertheless, let every one of you so love his own wife, even as himself.

Likewise the same Saint Paul (writing to the Colossians) speaketh thus to all men that be married: Ye men, love your wives and be not bitter unto them. *Coloss. iii.*

Hear also what saint Peter the apostle of Christ, (which was himself a married man.) saith unto all men that are married. Ye husbands, dwell with your wives according to knowledge: giving honour unto the wife, as unto the weaker vessel, and as heirs together of the grace of life, so that your prayers be not hindered. *1 Pet. iii.*

> Hitherto ye have heard the duty of the husband toward the wife.
>
> Now likewise, ye wives, hear and learn your duty toward your husbands, even as it is plainly set forth in holy scripture.

Saint Paul (in the forenamed Epistle to the Ephesians) teacheth you thus: Ye women submit yourselves unto your own husbands as unto the Lord: for the husband is the wife's head, even as Christ is the head of the church: And he also is the Saviour of the whole body. Therefore as the church, or congregation, is subject unto Christ: so likewise let the wives also be in subjection unto their own husbands in all things And again he saith: Let the wife reverence her husband. And in his Epistle to the Colossians Saint Paul giveth you this short lesson: Ye wives, submit yourselves unto your own husbands, as it is convenient in the Lord. *Ephes. v.* *Coloss. iii.*

Saint Peter also doth instruct you very godly, thus saying: Let wives ͫ be subject to their own husbands, so that if any obey not the word, they may be won without the word, by the conversa- *1 Pet. iii.*

ͫ In some copies, "let the wives."

tion of the wives; while they behold your chaste conversation, coupled with fear: whose apparel let it not be outward, with broided hair, and trimming about with gold, either in putting on of gorgeous apparel: But let the hid man, which is in the heart, be without all corruption, so that the spirit be mild and quiet, which is a precious thing in the sight of God. For after this manner (in the old time) did the holy women, which trusted in God, apparel themselves, being subject to their own husbands: as Sara obeyed Abraham calling him lord, whose daughters ye are made, doing well and being not dismayed with any fear.

The new married persons (the same day of their marriage) must receive the holy communion.

THE ORDER FOR THE
VISITATION OF THE SICK,
AND THE COMMUNION OF THE SAME.

¶ *The Priest entering into the sick person's house, shall say,*

PEACE be in this house, and to all that dwell in it.

When he cometh into the sick man's presence, he shall say this Psalm.

HEAR my prayer, (O Lord,) and consider my desire : hearken unto me for thy truth and righteousness' sake. *Domine exaudi. Psalm cxliii.*

And enter not into judgement with thy servant : for in thy sight shall no man living be justified.

For the enemy hath persecuted my soul; he hath smitten my life down to the ground : he hath laid me in the darkness, as the men that have been long dead.

Therefore is my spirit vexed within me : and my heart within me is desolate.

Yet do I remember the time past; I muse upon all thy works : yea, I exercise myself in the works of thy hands.

I stretch forth mine hands unto thee : my soul gaspeth unto thee as a thirsty land.

Hear me, (O lord,) and that soon, for my spirit waxeth faint : hide not thy face from me, lest I be like unto them that go down into the pit.

O let me hear thy loving-kindness betimes in the morning, for in thee is my trust : shew thou me the way that I should walk in, for I lift up my soul unto thee.

Deliver me, (O lord,) from mine enemies : for I fly unto thee to hide me.

Teach me to do the thing that pleaseth thee, for thou art my god, let thy loving spirit lead me forth unto the land of righteousness.

Quicken me, (O lord,) for thy name's sake, and for thy righteousness' sake bring my soul out of trouble.

And of thy goodness slay mine enemies : and destroy all them that vex my soul; for I am thy servant.

Glory to the father, and to the son, &c.

As it was in the beginning, &c.

¶ *With this anthem.*

REMEMBER not, Lord, our iniquities, nor the iniquities of our forefathers. Spare us, good Lord, spare thy people, whom thou hast redeemed with thy most precious blood, and be not angry with us for ever.

Lord, have mercy upon us.
Christ, have mercy upon us.
Lord, have mercy upon us.
Our Father, which art in heaven, &c.
And lead us not into temptation.
Answer. But deliver us from evil. Amen.
The Minister. O Lord, save thy servant.
Answer. Which putteth his trust in thee.
Minister. Send him help from thy holy place.
Answer. And evermore mightily defend him.
Minister. Let the enemy have none advantage of him.
Answer. Nor the wicked approach to hurt him.
Minister. Be unto him, O Lord, a strong tower.
Answer. From the face of his enemy.
Minister. Lord, hear my prayer.
Answer. And let my cry come unto thee.

Minister. Let us pray.

O LORD, look down from heaven, behold, visit, and relieve this thy servant: Look upon him with the eyes of thy mercy, give him comfort, and sure confidence in thee: Defend him from the danger of the enemy, and keep him in perpetual peace, and safety: through Jesus Christ our Lord. Amen.

Hear us, Almighty and most merciful God and Saviour: extend thy accustomed goodness to this thy servant, which is grieved with sickness: Visit him, O Lord, as thou didst visit Peter's wife's mother and the Captain's servant. And as thou preservedst Thobie and Sara by thy Angel from danger: So restore unto this sick person his former health, (if it be thy will,) or else give him grace so to take thy correction, that after this painful life ended, he may dwell with thee in life everlasting. Amen.

Then shall the Minister exhort the sick person after this form, or other like.

DEARLY beloved, know this, that Almighty God is the Lord over life, and death, and over all things to them pertaining, as youth, strength, health, age, weakness, and sickness. Wherefore, whatsoever your sickness is, know you certainly, that it is God's visitation. And for what cause soever this sickness is sent unto you; whether it be to try your patience for the example of other, and that your faith may be found, in the day of the Lord, laudable, glorious, and honourable, to the increase of glory, and endless felicity: or else it be sent unto you to correct and amend in you, whatsoever doth offend the eyes of our heavenly Father: know you certainly, that if you truly repent you of your sins, and bear your sickness patiently, trusting in God's mercy, for his dear Son Jesus Christ's sake, and render unto him humble thanks for his fatherly visitation, submitting yourself wholly to his will; it shall turn to your profit, and help you forward in the right way that leadeth unto everlasting life *. Take therefore in good worth the chastement of the Lord: for whom the Lord loveth he chastiseth. Yea, (as Saint Paul saith,) he scourgeth every son, which he receiveth: if you endure chastisement, he offereth himself unto you as unto his own children. What son is he that the father chastiseth not? If ye be not under correction (whereof all the true children are partakers), then are ye bastards, and not children.

* If the person visited be very sick, then the Curate may end his exhortation at this place ꜱ.

Therefore seeing that when our carnal fathers do correct us, we reverently obey them, shall we not now much rather be obedient to our spiritual Father, and so live? And they for a few days do chastise us after their own pleasure: but he doth chastise us for our profit, to the intent he may make us partakers of his holiness. These words, good brother, are God's words, and written in holy scripture for our comfort and instruction, that we should patiently and with thanksgiving bear our heavenly Father's correction, whensoever by any manner of adversity it shall please his gracious goodness to visit us. And there should be no greater comfort to christian persons, than to be made like unto Christ, by suffering patiently adversities, troubles, and sicknesses. For he himself went not up to joy, but first he suffered pain: he entered not into his glory, before he was crucified. So truly our way to eternal joy is to suffer here with Christ, and our door to enter into eternal life is gladly to die with Christ, that we may rise again from death, and dwell with him in everlasting life. Now therefore taking your sickness, which is thus profitable for you, patiently: I exhort you in the name of God, to remember the profession which you made unto God in your Baptism. And forasmuch as after this life there is account to be given unto

ꜱ In some copies the note is *omitted*.

THE VISITATION OF THE SICK.   137

the righteous Judge, of whom all must be judged without respect of persons : I require you to examine yourself and your state, both toward God and man, so that accusing and condemning yourself for your own faults, you may find mercy at our heavenly Father's hand, for Christ's sake, and not be accused and condemned in that fearful judgment. Therefore I shall shortly rehearse the articles of our faith, that ye may know whether you do believe as a christian man should believe or no.

Here the minister shall rehearse the articles of the faith, saying thus.

DOST thou believe in God the Father Almighty?

And so forth, as it is in Baptism.

Then shall the minister examine whether he be in charity with all the world: Exhorting him to forgive from the bottom of his heart all persons that have offended him: and if he have offended other to ask them forgiveness: and where he hath done injury or wrong to any man, that he make amends to his uttermost power. And if he have not afore disposed his goods, let him then make his will. (But men must be oft admonished that they set an order for their temporal goods and lands when they be in health.) And also to declare his debts, what he oweth, and what is owing unto[h] *him: for*[i] *discharging of his conscience, and quietness of his executors.* The minister may not forget nor omit to move the sick person (and that most earnestly) to liberality toward the poor.*

* This may be done before the minister begin his prayers, as he shall see cause.

¶ *Here shall the sick person make a special confession, if he feel his conscience troubled with any weighty matter. After which confession, the Priest shall absolve him after this form. And the same form of absolution shall be used in all private confessions.*

OUR Lord Jesus Christ, who hath left power to his Church to absolve all sinners, which truly repent and

---

[h] In some copies, "to."   [i] In some copies, "for" *omitted.*

believe in him, of his great mercy forgive thee thine offences: and by his authority committed to me, I absolve thee from all thy sins, in the name of the Father[k], and of the Son, and of the Holy Ghost. Amen.

And then the Priest shall say the Collect following.

Let us pray.

O MOST merciful God, which according to the multitude of thy mercies dost so put away the sins of those which truly repent, that thou rememberest them no more: open thy eye of mercy upon this thy servant, who most earnestly desireth pardon and forgiveness: Renew in him, most loving Father, whatsoever hath been decayed by the fraud[l] and malice of the devil, or by his own carnal will, and frailness: preserve and continue this sick member in the unity of thy Church, consider his contrition, accept his tears, assuage his pain, as shall be seen to thee most expedient for him. And forasmuch as he putteth his full trust only in thy mercy: Impute not unto him his former sins, but take him unto thy favour: through the merits of thy most dearly beloved Son Jesus Christ. Amen.

Then the Minister shall say this Psalm.

IN thee, O Lord, have I put my trust, let me never be put to confusion, but rid me, and deliver me, into thy righteousness: incline thine ear unto me, and save me. *In te Domine speravi.* Psal. 71.[m]

Be thou my strong hold, (whereunto I may alway resort) thou hast promised to help me: for thou art my house of defence, and my castle.

Deliver me (O my God) out of the hand of the un-

---

[k] In some copies the doxology stops here, and an "&c." added.
[l] In some copies, "defraud."
[m] In one ed. 1549, the reference is printed as Psal. 21, and this error is followed through all editions of 1552 and 1559.

godly, out of the hand of the unrighteous and cruel man.

For thou (O Lord God) art the thing that I long for, thou art my hope, even from my youth.

Through thee have I been holden up ever since I was born, thou art he that took me out of my mother's womb; my praise shall be always of thee.

I am become as it were a monster unto many: but my sure trust is in thee.

O let my mouth be filled with thy praise (that I may sing of thy glory) and honour all the day long.

Cast me not away in the time of age, forsake me not when my strength faileth me.

For mine enemies speak against me: and they that lay wait for my soul take their counsel together, saying: God hath forsaken him; persecute him, and take him, for there is none to deliver him.

Go not far from me, O God: my God, haste thee to help me.

Let them be confounded and perish that are against my soul: let them be covered with shame and dishonour that seek to do me evil.

As for me, I will patiently abide alway, and will praise thee more and more.

My mouth shall daily speak of thy righteousness and salvation, for I know no end thereof.

I will go forth in the strength of the Lord God: and will make mention of thy righteousness only.

Thou (O God) hast taught me from my youth up until now, therefore will I tell of thy wondrous works.

Forsake me not (O God) in mine old age, when I am gray-headed, until I have shewed thy strength unto this generation, and thy power to all them that are yet for to come.

Thy righteousness (O God) is very high, and great things are they that thou hast done: O God, who is like unto thee?

O what great troubles and adversities hast thou

shewed me! and yet didst thou turn and refresh me: yea, and broughtest me from the deep of the earth again.

Thou hast brought me to great honour, and comforted me on every side.

Therefore will I praise thee and thy faithfulness (O God) playing upon an instrument of musick, unto thee will I sing upon the harp, O thou holy one of Israel.

My lips will be fain when I sing unto thee: and so will my soul whom thou hast delivered.

My tongue also shall talk of thy righteousness all the day long, for they are confounded and brought unto shame that seek to do me evil.

Glory to the Father, &c.

As it was in the beginning, &c.

Adding this Anthem.

O SAVIOUR of the world, save us, which by thy cross and precious blood hast redeemed us, help us we beseech thee, O God.

Then shall the minister say,

THE Almighty Lord, which is a most strong tower to all them that put their trust in him, to whom all things in heaven, in earth, and under earth [n], do bow and obey: be now and evermore thy defence, and make thee know and feel, that there is no other name under heaven given to man, in whom and through whom thou mayest receive health and salvation, but only the name of our Lord Jesus Christ. Amen.

¶ *If the sick person desire to be anointed, then shall the Priest anoint him upon the forehead or breast only, making the sign of the cross, saying thus,*

AS with this visible oil thy body outwardly is anointed: so our heavenly Father, Almighty God, grant of his infinite goodness, that thy soul inwardly

---

[n] In some copies, "under the earth."

may be anointed with the Holy Ghost, who is the Spirit of all strength, comfort, relief, and gladness: and vouchsafe for his great mercy (if it be his blessed will) to restore unto thee thy bodily health, and strength, to serve him ; and send thee release of all thy pains, troubles, and diseases, both in body and mind. And howsoever his goodness (by his divine and unsearchable providence) shall dispose of thee : we, his unworthy ministers and servants, humbly beseech the eternal majesty to do with thee according to the multitude of his innumerable mercies, and to pardon thee all thy sins and offences, committed by all thy bodily senses, passions, and carnal affections : who also vouchsafe mercifully to grant unto thee ghostly strength, by his Holy Spirit, to withstand and overcome all temptations and assaults of thine adversary, that in no wise he prevail against thee, but that thou mayest have perfect victory and triumph against the devil, sin, and death, through Christ our Lord: Who by his death hath overcomed ° the prince of death, and with the Father and the Holy Ghost evermore liveth and reigneth God, world without end. Amen.

How long wilt thou forget me, (O Lord,) for ever ? how long wilt thou hide thy face from me? How long shall I seek counsel in my soul? and be so vexed in mine heart? how long shall mine enemy triumph over me? Consider, and hear me, (O lord my God) : lighten mine eyes, that I sleep not in death. Lest mine enemy say, I have prevailed against him : for if I be cast down, they that trouble me will rejoice at it. But my trust is in thy mercy : and my heart is joyful in thy salvation. I will sing of the lord, because he hath dealt so lovingly with me : yea, I will praise the Name of the Lord the most Highest. Glory to the, &c. As it was in the, &c. *Usque quo, Domine. Psalm xiii.*

° In some copies, "overcome."

THE COMMUNION OF THE SICK.

Forasmuch as all mortal men be subject to many sudden perils, diseases, and sicknesses[p], *and ever uncertain what time they shall depart out of this life: Therefore to the intent they may be always in a readiness to die, whensoever it shall please Almighty God to call them, the curates shall diligently from time to time, but specially in the plague time, exhort their parishioners to the oft receiving (in the church) of the holy Communion of the body and blood of our Saviour Christ: which if they do, they shall have no cause, in their sudden visitation, to be unquieted for lack of the same. But if the sick person be not able to come to the church, and yet is desirous to receive the Communion in his house, then he must give knowledge over night, or else early in the morning to the curate, signifying also how many be appointed to communicate with him. And if the same day there be a celebration of the Holy Communion in the church, then shall the Priest reserve (at the open Communion) so much of the sacrament of the body and blood, as shall serve the sick person, and so many as shall communicate with him (if there be any); and so soon as he conveniently may, after the open Communion ended in the church, shall go and minister the same, first to those that are appointed to communicate with the sick (if there be any), and last of all to the sick person himself. But before the curate distribute the holy Communion, the appointed* general confession must be made in the name of the communicants, the curate adding the *absolution with the comfortable sentences of scripture following in the open Communion: and after the communion ended, the Collect.*

ALMIGHTY and everliving God, we most heartily thank thee, &c.

¶ *But if the day be not appointed for the open communion in the church, then (upon convenient warning given) the curate shall come and visit the sick person afore noon. And*

---

[p] In some copies, "sickness."

having a convenient place in the sick man's house (where he may reverently celebrate) with all things necessary for the same, and not being otherwise letted with the public service or any other just impediment; he shall there celebrate the holy communion after such form and sort as hereafter is appointed.

THE CELEBRATION
of the Holy Communion for the Sick.

O PRAISE the Lord, all ye nations, laud him, all ye people: for his merciful kindness is confirmed toward us, and the truth of the Lord endureth for ever.

Glory be to the Father, and to the Son, &c.

Lord, have mercy upon us.
Christ, have mercy upon us. } Without any more repetition.
Lord, have mercy upon us.

The Priest. The Lord be with you
Answer. And with thy spirit.

Let us pray.

ALMIGHTY everliving God, maker of mankind, which dost correct those whom thou dost love, and chastisest every one whom thou dost receive: we beseech thee to have mercy upon this thy servant visited with thy hand, and to grant that he may take his sickness patiently, and recover his bodily health (if it be thy gracious will), and whensoever his soul shall depart from the body, it may without spot be presented unto thee: through Jesus Christ our Lord. Amen.

The Epistle.

MY son, despise not the correction of the Lord, neither faint when thou art rebuked of him: for whom the Lord loveth, him he correcteth, yea and he scourgeth every son, whom he receiveth. Heb. xii.

The Gospel.

VERILY, verily I say unto you, He that heareth my word, and believeth on him that sent me, hath everlasting life, and shall not come unto damnation, but he passeth from death unto life. *John v.*

The Preface.

The Lord be with you.
Answer. And with thy spirit.
¶ Lift up your hearts, &c.

Unto the end of the Canon.

¶ *At the time of the distribution of the holy sacrament, the priest shall first receive the Communion himself, and after minister to them that be appointed to Communicate with the sick (if there be any), and then to the sick person. And the sick person shall always desire some, either of his own house, or else of his neighbours, to receive the holy Communion with him; for that shall be to him a singular great comfort, and of their part a great token of charity.*

¶ *And if there be more sick persons to be visited the same day that the curate doth celebrate in any sick man's house; then shall the curate (there) reserve so much of the sacrament of the body*[q] *and blood, as shall serve the other sick persons, and such as be appointed to communicate with them (if there be any); and shall immediately carry it, and minister it unto them.*

¶ *But if any man either by reason of extremity of sickness, or for lack of warning given in due time to the curate, or by any other just impediment, do not receive the sacrament of Christ's body and blood; then the curate shall instruct him, that if he do truly repent him of his sins, and stedfastly believe that Jesus Christ hath suffered death upon the cross for him, and shed his blood for his redemption, earnestly remembering the benefits he hath thereby, and giving him hearty thanks therefore; he doth eat and drink spiritually the body and blood of our Saviour Christ, profitably to his soul's health, although he do not receive the sacrament with his mouth.*

[q] In some copies, "Christ's body."

THE COMMUNION OF THE SICK.

¶ *When the sick person is visited and receiveth the holy Communion all at one time: then the priest for more expedition shall use this order at the visitation.*

The Anthem.

Remember not, Lord, &c.
Lord, have mercy upon us.
Christ, have mercy upon us.
Lord, have mercy upon us.
¶ Our Father which art in heaven, &c.
And lead us not into temptation.
Answer. But deliver us from evil. Amen.

Let us pray.
O Lord[r], look down from heaven, &c.[s]

With the first part of the exhortation and all other things unto the Psalm,

In thee, O Lord, have I put my trust, &c.

And if the sick desire to be anointed, then shall the priest use the appointed prayer without any Psalm.

---

[r] In some copies, "Lord" *omitted.*   [s] In some copies, "&c." *omitted.*

THE ORDER FOR THE BURIAL OF THE DEAD.

The priest meeting the corpse at the church stile, shall say: Or else the priests and clerks shall sing, and so go either into the church, or towards ᵗ *the grave.*

I AM the resurrection and the life (saith the Lord): he that believeth in me, yea though he were dead, yet shall he live. And whosoever liveth and believeth in me, shall not die for ever.   John xi.

I KNOW that my Redeemer liveth, and that I shall rise out of the earth in the last day, and shall be covered again with my skin, and shall see God in my flesh: yea and I myself shall behold him, not with other but with these same eyes.   Job xix.ᵘ

WE brought nothing into this world, neither may we carry any thing out of this world. The Lord giveth, and the Lord taketh away. Even as it pleaseth the Lord, so cometh things to pass: blessed be the name of the Lord.   1 Tim. vi.   Job i.

When they come at the grave, whiles the corpse is made ready to be laid into the earth, the priest shall say, or else the priest and clerks shall sing.

MAN that is born of a woman, hath but a short time to live, and is full of misery: he cometh up and is cut down like a flower; he flieth as it were a shadow, and never continueth in one stay.   Job ix.ˣ

¶ In the midst of life we be in death: of whom may we seek for succour, but of thee, O Lord, which for our sins justly art moved? Yet O Lordʸ God

---

ᵗ In some copies, "toward."   ᵘ In some copies, *mispr.* John xix.
ˣ This is a misprint for Job xiv., but it occurs in all the copies.   ʸ In some copies, the line, "which for our sins justly art moved? Yet, O Lord," is accidentally *omitted.*

AT THE BURIAL.

most holy, O Lord most mighty, O holy and most merciful Saviour, deliver us not into the bitter pains of eternal death. Thou knowest, Lord, the secrets of our hearts: shut not up thy merciful eyes to our prayers: But spare us, Lord most holy, O God most mighty, O holy and merciful Saviour, thou most worthy Judge eternal, suffer us not at our last hour for any pains of death to fall from thee.

Then the priest casting earth upon the corpse, shall say,

I COMMEND thy soul to God the Father Almighty, and thy body to the ground, earth to earth, ashes to ashes, dust to dust, in sure and certain hope of resurrection to eternal life, through our Lord Jesus Christ, who shall change our vile body, that it may be like to his glorious body, according to the mighty working whereby he is able to subdue all things to himself.

Then shall be said or sung,

I HEARD a voice from heaven, saying unto me: Write, blessed are the dead which die in Lord. Even so saith the Spirit, that they rest from their labours. *Apoc. xiv.*

Let us pray.

WE commend into thy hands of mercy, most merciful Father, the soul of this our brother departed, *N.* And his body we commit to the earth, beseeching thine infinite goodness, to give us grace to live in thy fear and love, and to die in thy favour: that when the judgment shall come which thou hast committed to thy well beloved Son, both this our brother, and we, may be found acceptable in thy sight, and receive that blessing, which thy well beloved Son shall then pronounce to all that love and fear thee, saying, Come, ye blessed children of my Father: Receive the kingdom prepared for you before the beginning of the world. Grant this, merciful Father, for the honour of Jesu Christ our only Saviour, Mediator, and Advocate. Amen.

This prayer shall also be added.

ALMIGHTY God, we give thee hearty thanks for this thy servant, whom thou hast delivered from the miseries of this wretched world, from the body of death and all temptation; and, as we trust, hast brought his soul, which he committed into thy holy hands, into sure consolation and rest: Grant, we beseech thee, that at the day of judgment his soul and all the souls of thy elect, departed out of this life, may with us, and we with them, fully receive thy promises, and be made perfit altogether, thorough the glorious resurrection of thy Son Jesus Christ our Lord.

These psalms with other suffrages following are to be said in the church, either before or after the burial of the corpse.

I AM well pleased that the Lord hath heard the voice of my prayer.

That he hath inclined his ear unto me, therefore will I call upon him as long as I live. *Dilexi, quoniam. Psalm cxvi.*[1]

The snares of death compassed me round about, and the pains of hell gat hold upon me: I shall find trouble and heaviness, and I shall call upon the Name of the Lord, (O Lord), I beseech thee deliver my soul.

Gracious is the Lord, and righteous, yea, our God is merciful.

The Lord preserveth the simple: I was in misery, and he helped me.

Turn again then unto thy rest, O my soul, for the Lord hath rewarded thee.

And why? thou hast delivered my soul from death, mine eyes from tears, and my feet from falling.

---

[1] In some copies, *mispr.* Psalm clxxvi.

I will walk before the Lord, in the land of the living.

I believed, and therefore will I speak : but I was sore troubled. I said in my haste : all men are liars.

What reward shall I give unto the Lord for all the benefits that he hath done unto me?

I will receive the cup of salvation, and call upon the Name of the Lord.

I will pay my vows now in the presence of all his people : right dear in the sight of the Lord is the death of his Saints.

Behold (O Lord) how that I am thy servant : I am thy servant, and the son of thy handmaid, thou hast broken my bonds in sunder.

I will offer to thee the sacrifice of thanksgiving, and will call upon the Name of the Lord.

I will pay my vows unto the Lord, in the sight of all his people, in the courts of the Lord's house, even in the midst of thee, O Hierusalem.

Glory be to the Father, &c.

As it was in the beginning, &c.

PRAISE the Lord, (O my soul), while I live will I praise the Lord : yea, as long as I have any being, I will sing praises unto my God. *Lauda, anima, mea.* Psal. cxlvi.

O put not your trust in princes, nor in any child of man, for there is no help in them. ☞ *Note that this Psalm is to be said after the others that followeth*[a].

For when the breath of man goeth forth, he shall turn again to his earth, and then all his thoughts perish.

Blessed is he that hath the God of Jacob for his help : and whose hope is in the Lord his God.

Which made heaven and earth, the sea, and all that therein is : which keepeth his promise for ever.

---

[a] This appears thus in most copies; in some few the psalms are printed in the order in which they should be read.

Which helpeth them to right that suffer wrong, which feedeth the hungry.

The Lord looseth men out of prison, the Lord giveth sight to the blind.

The Lord helpeth them up that are fallen, the Lord careth for the righteous.

The Lord careth for the strangers, he defendeth the fatherless and widow : as for the way of the ungodly, he turneth it upside down.

The Lord thy God, O Sion, shall be King for evermore, and throughout all generations.

Glory be to the Father, &c.

As it was in the beginning, &c.

O LORD, thou hast searched me out, and known me. *Domine, probasti.* Psalm cxxxix.

Thou knowest my down-sitting, and mine uprising : thou understandest my thoughts long before.

Thou art about my path, and about my bed, and spiest out all my ways.

For lo, there is not a word in my tongue, but thou (O Lord) knowest it altogether.

Thou hast fashioned me, behind and before, and laid thine hand upon me.

Such knowledge is too wonderful and excellent for me : I cannot attain unto it.

Whither shall I go then from thy Spirit? or whither shall I go then from thy presence ?

If I climb up into heaven, thou art there : if I go down to hell, thou art there also.

If I take the wings of the morning, and remain in the uttermost parts of the sea ;

Even there also shall thy hand lead me, and thy right hand shall hold me.

If I say : peradventure the darkness shall cover me, then shall my night be turned to day.

Yea, the darkness is no darkness with thee : but

the night is all clear as the day, the darkness and light to thee are both alike.

For my reins are thine, thou hast covered me in my mother's womb : I will give thanks unto thee, for I am fearfully and wonderfully made : marvellous are thy works, and that my soul knoweth right well.

My bones are not hid from thee, though I be made secretly, and fashioned beneath in the earth.

Thine eyes did see my substance, yet being unperfect : and in thy book were all my members written ;

Which day by day were fashioned, when as yet there was none of them.

How dear are thy counsels unto me, O God? O how great is the sum of them?

If I tell them, they are more in number than the sand : when I wake up, I am present with thee.

Wilt thou not slay the wicked, O God? depart from me, ye blood-thirsty men.

For they speak unrighteously against thee : and thine enemies take thy Name in vain.

Do not I hate them, O Lord, that hate thee : and am not I grieved with those that rise up against thee?

Yea, I hate them right sore? even as though they were mine enemies.

Try me, O God, and seek the ground of mine heart : prove me, and examine my thoughts.

Look well if there be any way of wickedness in me, and lead me in the way everlasting.

Glory be to the Father, &c.

As it was in the beginning, &c.

Then shall follow this lesson, taken out of the fifteenth chapter to the Corinthians, the first Epistle.

CHRIST is risen from the dead, and become the firstfruits of them that slept. For by a man came death, and by a man came the resurrection of the dead. For as by Adam all die, even so   1 Cor. 15.

by Christ shall all be made alive, but every man in his own order. The first is Christ, then they that are Christ's, at his coming. Then cometh the end, when he hath delivered up the kingdom to God the Father, when he hath put down all rule and all authority and power. For he must reign till he have put all his enemies under his feet. The last enemy that shall be destroyed is death. For he hath put all things under his feet. But when he saith all things are put under him, it is manifest that he is excepted, which did put all things under him. When all things are subdued unto him, then shall the Son also himself be subject unto him that put all things under him, that God may be all in all. Else what do they which are baptized over the dead, if the dead rise not at all? Why are they then baptized over them? yea and why stand we alway then in jeopardy? By our rejoicing, which I have in Christ Jesu our Lord, I die daily. That I have fought with beasts at Ephesus after the manner of men, what advantageth it me, if the dead rise not again? Let us eat, and drink, for to-morrow we shall die. Be not ye deceived: evil words corrupt good manners. Awake truly out of sleep, and sin not. For some have not the knowledge of God. I speak this to your shame. But some man will say: How arise the dead? with what body shall they come? Thou fool, that which thou sowest is not quickened, except it die. And what sowest thou? Thou sowest not that body that shall be; but bare corn as of wheat, or of some other: but God giveth it a body at his pleasure, to every seed his own body. All flesh is not one manner of flesh : but there is one manner of flesh of men, another manner of flesh of beasts, another of fishes, another of birds. There are also celestial bodies, and there are bodies terrestrial. But the glory of the celestial is one, and the glory of the terrestrial is another. There is one manner glory of the sun, and another glory of the moon, and another glory of the stars. For one star differeth from another in glory. So is the resurrection of the dead. It is sown in corruption, it riseth again in incorruption. It is sown in dishonour, it riseth again in honour. It is sown in weakness, it riseth again in power. It is sown a natural body, it riseth again a spiritual body. There is a natural body, and there is a spiritual body: as it is also written: The first man Adam was made a living soul, and the last Adam was made a quickening Spirit. Howbeit, that is not first which is spiritual: but that which is natural, and then that which is spiritual. The first man is of the earth, earthy: the second man is the Lord from heaven (heavenly). As is the earthy, such are they that are earthy. And as is the heavenly, such are they that are heavenly. And as we have borne the image of the earthy, so shall we bear the image of the heavenly. This say I, brethren, that flesh and blood cannot inherit the kingdom of God: neither doth corruption inherit uncorruption. Behold, I shew you a mystery. We shall not all sleep: but we shall all be changed and that in a moment, in the twinkling of an eye by the last trump. For the trump shall blow, and the dead shall rise incorruptible, and we shall be changed. For this corruptible must put on incorruption: and this mortal must put on immortality. When this corruptible hath put on incorruption, and this mortal hath put on immortality: then shall be brought to pass the saying that is written: Death is swallowed up in victory: Death, where is thy sting? Hell, where is thy victory? The sting of death is sin: and the strength of sin is the law. But thanks be unto God which hath given us victory, through our Lord Jesus Christ. Therefore, my dear brethren, be ye stedfast, and unmoveable, always rich in the work of the Lord, forasmuch as ye know that your labour is not in vain in the Lord.

The lesson ended, then shall the Priest say,

Lord, have mercy upon us.
Christ, have mercy upon us.
Lord, have mercy upon us.
Our Father which art in heaven, &c.
And lead us not into temptation.
Answer. But deliver us from evil. Amen.
Priest. Enter not (O Lord) into judgment with thy servant.
Answer. For in thy sight no living creature shall be justified.
Priest. From the gates of hell.
Answer. Deliver their souls, O Lord.
Priest. I believe to see the goodness of the Lord.
Answer. In the land of the living.
Priest. O Lord, graciously hear my prayer.
Answer. And let my cry come unto thee.

Let us pray.

O LORD, with whom do live the spirits of them that be dead: and in whom the souls of them that be elected, after they be delivered from the burden of the flesh, be in joy and felicity: Grant unto this thy servant, that the sins which he committed in this world be not imputed unto him, but that he, escaping the gates of hell, and pains of eternal darkness, may ever dwell in the region of light, with Abraham, Isaac, and Jacob, in the place where is no weeping, sorrow, nor heaviness; and when that dreadful day of the general resurrection shall come, make him to rise also with the just and righteous, and receive this body again to glory, then made pure and incorruptible: set him on the right hand of thy Son Jesus Christ, among thy holy and elect, that then he may hear with them these most sweet and comfortable words: Come to me, ye blessed of my Father, possess the kingdom which hath been prepared for you from the beginning of the world: Grant this, we beseech thee, O merciful Father, through Jesus Christ our Mediator and Redeemer. Amen.

THE CELEBRATION

of the holy communion when there is a burial of the dead.

LIKE as the hart desireth the water-brooks, so longeth my soul after thee, O God. *Quemadmodum* Psalm xlii.

My soul is athirst for God, yea, even for the living God: when shall I come to appear before the presence of God?

My tears have been my meat day and night, while they daily say unto me, Where is now thy God?

Now when I think thereupon, I pour out my heart by myself: for I went with the multitude, and brought them forth unto the house of God, in the voice of praise and thanksgiving, among such as keep holy-day.

Why art thou so full of heaviness, (O my soul): and why art thou so unquiet within me?

Put thy trust in God, for I will yet give him thanks for the help of his countenance.

My God, my soul is vexed within me: therefore will I remember thee concerning the land of Jordan, and the little hill of Hermonim.

One deep calleth another, because of thy noise of thy water-pipes, all thy waves and storms are gone over me.

The Lord hath granted his loving-kindness on the day-time, and in the night-season did I sing of him, and made my prayer unto the God of my life.

I will say unto the God of my strength, why hast thou forgotten me? why go I thus heavily, while the enemy oppresseth me?

My bones are smitten asunder, while mine enemies

(that trouble me) cast me in the teeth, namely, while they say daily unto me: where is now thy God?

Why art thou so vexed, (O my soul) and why art thou so disquieted within me?

O put thy trust in God, for I will yet thank him which is the help of my countenance, and my God.

Glory to the Father, &c.

As it was in the beginning, &c.

The Collect[b].

O MERCIFUL God the Father of our Lord Jesu Christ, who is the resurrection and the life: In whom whosoever believeth shall live, though he die: and whosoever liveth, and believeth in him, shall not die eternally: who also hath taught us (by his holy apostle Paul) not to be sorry as men without hope for them that sleep in him: We meekly beseech thee (O Father) to raise us from the death of sin unto the life of righteousness, that when we shall depart this life, we may sleep in him (as our hope is this our brother doth), and at the general resurrection in the last day both we and this our brother departed, receiving again our bodies, and rising again in thy most gracious favour, may with all thine elect Saints obtain eternal joy. Grant this, O Lord God, by the means of our Advocate Jesus Christ: which with thee and the Holy Ghost, liveth and reigneth one God for ever. Amen.

The Epistle.

I WOULD not, brethren, that ye should be ignorant concerning them which are fallen asleep, that ye sorrow not, as other do, which have no hope. For if we believe that Jesus died and rose again: even so them also which sleep by Jesus, will God bring again with him. For this say we unto you in the word of the Lord, that we which shall live, and shall remain in the coming of the Lord, shall not

1 Thess. iv.

---

[b] In some copies, "Collect."

come ere they which sleep. For the Lord himself shall descend from heaven with a shout, and the voice of the archangel, and trump of God: and the dead in Christ shall rise first: Then we which shall live (even we shall remain) shall be caught up with them also in the clouds, to meet the Lord in the air: and so shall we ever be with the Lord. Wherefore comfort yourselves one another with these words.

¶ *The Gospel.*

Jesus said to his disciples and to the Jews: All that the Father giveth me shall come to me: and he that cometh to me I shall not cast away. For I came down from heaven: not to do that I will, but that he will, which hath sent me. And this is the Father's will which hath sent me, that of all which he hath given me, I shall lose nothing: but raise them up again at the last day. And this is the will of him that sent me: that every one which seeth the son and believeth on him, have everlasting life: And I will raise him up at the last day.

John vi.

THE ORDER OF THE PURIFICATION OF WOMEN.

The woman shall come into the church, and there shall kneel down in some convenient place, nigh unto the quire door: and the Priest standing by her shall say these words, or such like, as the case shall require.

FORASMUCH as it hath pleased Almighty God of his goodness to give you safe deliverance, and your child baptism, and hath preserved you in the great danger of childbirth: ye shall therefore give hearty thanks unto God, and pray.

Then shall the Priest say this Psalm.

I HAVE lifted up mine eyes unto the hills, from whence cometh my help? *Levavi oculos.*
My help cometh even from the Lord, Psalm cxxi.[e] which hath made heaven and earth.

He will not suffer thy foot to be moved, and he that keepeth thee will not sleep.

Behold, he that keepeth Israel, shall neither slumber nor sleep.

The Lord himself is thy keeper, the Lord is thy defence upon thy right hand.

So that the sun shall not burn thee by day, neither the moon by night.

The Lord shall preserve thee from all evil, yea, it is even he that shall keep thy soul.

The Lord shall preserve thy going out, **and thy coming in**, from this time forth for evermore.

Glory to the Father, &c.

As it was in the beginning, &c.

  Lord, have mercy upon us.
  Christ, have mercy upon us.
  Lord, have mercy upon us.

[e] In some copies, *misp.* Psalm xxi.

¶ Our Father which art in heaven, &c.
And lead us not into temptation.
Answer. But deliver us from evil. Amen.
Priest. O Lord, save this woman thy servant.
Answer. Which putteth her trust in thee.
Priest. Be thou to her a strong tower.
Answer. From the face of her enemy.
Priest. Lord [d], hear our prayer.
Answer. And let our cry come to thee.

Priest. ¶ Let us pray.

O ALMIGHTY God, which hast delivered this woman thy servant from the great pain and peril of childbirth: Grant, we beseech thee (most merciful Father), that she through thy help may both faithfully live, and walk in her vocation according to thy will in this life present; and also may be partaker of everlasting glory in the life to come: through Jesus Christ our Lord. Amen.

The woman that is purified, must offer her chrisom, and other accustomed offerings. And if there be a Communion, it is convenient that she receive the holy Communion.

[d] In some copies, "O Lord."

THE FIRST DAY OF LENT

COMMONLY CALLED

ASH-WEDNESDAY.

¶ *After Matins ended, the people being called together by the ringing of a bell, and assembled in the church, the English Litany shall be said after the accustomed manner*[e]*: which ended, the Priest shall go into the pulpit, and say thus:*

BRETHREN, in the primitive church there was a godly discipline, that at the beginning of Lent such persons as were notorious sinners, were put to open penance [f], and punished in this world, that their souls might be saved in the day of the Lord; and that other admonished by their example, might be more afraid to offend. In the stead whereof, until the said discipline may be restored again, (which thing is much to be wished,) it is thought good, that at this time (in your presence) should be read the general sentences of God's cursing against impenitent sinners, gathered out of the xxviith chapter of Deuteronomy, and other places of scripture: and that ye should answer to every sentence, Amen. To the intent that you being admonished of the great indignation of God against sinners, may the rather be called to earnest and true repentance, and may walk more warily in these dangerous days, fleeing [g] from such vices, for the which ye affirm with your own mouths the curse of God to be due.

[e] In some copies, "shall be said in such wise as in the end of this book is set forth, and in the accustomed places appointed by the King's injunctions."
[f] In some copies, the words, "put to open penance, and," are *omitted*.
[g] In some copies, "flying."

THE FIRST DAY OF LENT. 161

¶ CURSED is the man that maketh any carved or molten image, an abomination to the Lord, the work of the hands of the craftsman, and putteth it in a secret place to worship it.

And the people shall answer, and say,

Amen.

Minister. Cursed is he that curseth his father, and mother.

Answer. Amen.

Minister. Cursed is he that removeth away the mark of his neighbour's land.

Answer. Amen.

Minister. Cursed is he that maketh the blind to go out of his way.

Answer. Amen.

Minister. Cursed is he that letteth in judgment the right of the stranger, of them that be fatherless, and of widows.

Answer. Amen.

Minister. Cursed is he that smiteth his neighbour secretly.

Answer. Amen.

Minister. Cursed is he that lieth with his neighbour's wife.

Answer. Amen.

Minister. Cursed is he that taketh reward to slay the soul of innocent blood.

Answer. Amen.

Minister. Cursed is he that putteth his trust in man, and taketh man for his defence, and in his heart goeth from the Lord.

Answer. Amen.

Minister. Cursed are the unmerciful, the fornicators and advouterers, the covetous persons, the worshippers of images, slanderers, drunkards, and extortioners.

Answer. Amen.

The Minister. Now seeing that all they be accursed (as the prophet David beareth witness) which do err and go astray from the com- ^(Psal. cxviii.ᵇ) mandments of God, let us (remembering the dreadful judgment hanging over our heads, and being always at hand) return unto our Lord God, with all contrition and meekness of heart, bewailing and lamenting our sinful life, knowledging and confessing our offences, and seeking to bring forth worthy fruits of penance. For even now is the axe put ^(Mat. iii.) unto the root of the trees, so that every tree which bringeth not forth good fruit, is hewn down and cast into the fire. It is a fearful thing to fall into the hands of the living God: ^(Hebru. x.) ^(Psal. x.) he shall pour down rain upon the sinners, ^(Esai. xxvi.) snares, fire and brimstone, storm and tempest: this shall be their portion to drink. For lo, the Lord is coming out of his place, to visit the wickedness of such as dwell upon the earth. But ^(Mal. iii.ⁱ) who may abide the day of his coming? ^(Mat. iii.) Who shall be able to endure when he appeareth? His fan is in his hand, and he will purge his floor, and gather his wheat into the barn, but he will burn the chaff with unquenchable fire. The day of the Lord cometh as a thief upon the night; and when men shall say peace, and all things are safe, then shall sudden de- ^(1 Thess. v.ᵏ) struction come upon them, as sorrow cometh upon a woman travailing with child, and they shall not escape: then shall appear the wrath of God in the day of vengeance, which obstinate sinners, through the stubbornness of their heart, have heaped unto themself, which despised the goodness, patience and long-sufferance of God, when ^(Rom. ii.)

ᵇ In some copies, *mispr.* Ps. cxvii.   ⁱ In some copies, *mispr.* Mal. xxv.   ᵏ In some copies, reference *omitted*.

he called them continually to repentance. Then shall they call upon me (saith the Lord), but I will not hear: they shall seek me early, but they shall not find me, and that because they hated knowledge, and received not the fear of the Lord, but abhorred my counsel and despised my correction: then shall it be too late to knock, when the door shall be shut, and too late to cry for mercy, when it is the time of justice. O terrible voice of most just judgment, which shall be pronounced upon them, when it shall be said unto them, Go ye cursed into the fire everlasting, which is prepared for the devil and his angels. Therefore, brethren, take we heed betime, while the day of salvation lasteth, for the night cometh when none can work: but let us, while we have the light, believe in the light, and walk as the children of the light, that we be not cast into the utter darkness, where is weeping and gnashing of teeth. Let us not abuse the goodness of God, which calleth us mercifully to amendment, and of his endless pity promiseth us forgiveness of that which is past, if (with a whole mind and a true heart) we return unto him: for though our sins be red[m] as scarlet, they shall be as white as snow; and[n] though they be like purple, yet shall they be as white as wool. Turn you clean (saith the Lord) from all your wickedness, and your sin shall not be your destruction. Cast away from you all your ungodliness that ye have done, make you new hearts, and a new spirit: wherefore will ye die, O ye house of Israel, seeing I have no pleasure in the death of him that dieth? saith the Lord God. Turn you then, and you shall live. Although we have

Proverb. i.

Math. xxv.

2 Cor. vi. [1]
John ix.

Mat. xxv.

Esai. i.
Esech.
xviii.[o]

---

[1] In some copies, *mispr.* 1 Cor. vi.   [m] In some copies, "as red as."   [n] In some copies, "and" *omitted*.   [o] In some copies, *mispr.* Ezech. xvii.

sinned, yet have we an Advocate with the Father, Jesus Christ the righteous, and he it is that obtaineth grace for our sins; for he was wounded for our offences, and smitten for our wickedness: let us therefore return unto him, who is the merciful receiver of all true penitent sinners, assuring ourself that he is ready to receive us, and most willing to pardon us, if we come to him with faithful repentance: if we will submit ourselves unto him, and from henceforth walk in his ways: if we will take his easy yoke and light burden upon us to follow him in lowliness, patience, and charity, and be ordered by the governance of his holy Spirit, seeking always his glory, and serving him duly in our vocation with thanksgiving. This if we do, Christ will deliver us from the curse of the law, and from the extreme malediction which shall light upon them that shall be set on the left hand: and he will set us on his right hand, and give us the blessed benediction of his Father, commanding us to take possession of his glorious kingdom; unto the which he vouchsafe to bring us all, for his infinite mercy. Amen.

1 John ii.
Esai. liii.
Math. xi.
Math. xxv.

¶ *Then shall they all kneel upon their knees: and the Priest and clerks kneeling (where they are accustomed to say the Litany) shall say this psalm.*

HAVE mercy upon me, (O God,) after thy great goodness: according to the multitude of thy mercies, do away mine offences.

Wash me throughly from my wickedness, and cleanse me from my sin.

For I knowledge my faults, and my sin is ever before me.

Against thee only have I sinned, and done this evil in thy sight: that thou mightest be justified in thy saying, and clear when thou art judged.

Miserere mei Deus.
Psal. li.

THE FIRST DAY OF LENT. 165

Behold, I was shapen in wickedness, and in sin hath my mother conceived me.

But lo, thou requirest truth in the inward parts, and shalt make me to understand wisdom secretly.

Thou shalt purge me with hyssop, and I shall be clean : thou shalt wash me, and I shall be whiter than snow.

Thou shalt make me hear of joy and gladness, that the bones which thou hast broken may rejoice.

Turn thy face from my sins, and put out all my misdeeds.

Make me a clean heart, (O God) and renew a right spirit within me.

Cast me not away from thy presence, and take not thy holy Spirit from me.

O give me the comfort of thy help again, and stablish me with thy free spirit.

Then shall I teach thy ways unto the wicked, and sinners shall be converted unto thee.

Deliver me from blood-guiltiness, (O God,) thou that art the God of my health : and my tongue shall sing of thy righteousness.

Thou shalt open my lips, (O Lord) and my mouth shall shew thy praise.

For thou desirest no sacrifice, else would I give it thee : but thou delightest not in burnt-offering.

The sacrifice of God is a troubled spirit, a broken and contrite heart, (O God,) shalt thou not despise.

O be favourable and gracious unto Sion, build thou the walls of Jerusalem.

Then shalt thou be pleased with the sacrifice of righteousness, with the burnt-offerings and oblations : then shall they offer young bullocks upon thine altar.

Glory to the Father, &c.

As it was in the beginning, &c.

¶ Lord, have mercy upon us.
¶ Christ, have mercy upon us.
¶ Lord, have mercy upon us.

Our Father which art in heaven, &c.
And lead us not into temptation.
Answer. But deliver us from evil. Amen.
Minister. O Lord save thy servants.
Answer. Which put their trust in thee.
Minister. Send unto them help from above.
Answer. And evermore mightily defend them.
Minister. Help us, O God our Saviour.
Answer. And for the glory of thy name's sake deliver us, be merciful unto us sinners for thy name's sake.
Minister. O Lord, hear my prayer.
Answer. And let my cry come to thee.

Let us pray.

O LORD, we beseech thee mercifully hear our prayers, and spare all those which confess their sins to thee, that they whose consciences by sin are accused, by thy merciful pardon may be absolved, through Christ our Lord. Amen.

O MOST mighty God and merciful Father, which hast compassion of all men, and hatest nothing that thou hast made: which wouldest not the death of a sinner, but that he should rather turn from sin and be saved: mercifully forgive us our trespasses, receive and comfort us, which be grieved and wearied with the burden of our sin. Thy property is to have mercy, to thee only it appertaineth to forgive sins: spare us therefore, good Lord, spare thy people whom thou hast redeemed. Enter not into judgment with thy servants, which be vile earth, and miserable sinners: But so turn thy ire from us, which meekly knowledge our vileness, and truly repent us of our faults: so make haste to help us in this world, that we may ever live with thee in the world to come: through Jesus Christ our Lord. Amen.

THE FIRST DAY OF LENT.

Then shall this anthem be said or sung.

TURN thou us, good Lord, and so shall we be turned: be favourable (O Lord) be favourable to thy people, which turn to thee in weeping, fasting and praying: for thou art a merciful God, full of compassion, long suffering, and of a great pity[p]: Thou sparest when we deserve punishment, and in thy wrath thinkest upon mercy. Spare thy people, good Lord, spare them, and let not thine[q] heritage be brought to confusion: Hear us (O Lord) for thy mercy is great, and after the multitude of thy mercies look upon us.

[p] In some copies, "of a great piety." [q] In some copies, "thy heritage."

OF CEREMONIES,

WHY SOME BE ABOLISHED AND SOME RETAINED.

OF such ceremonies as be used in the Church, and have had their beginning by the institution of man: Some at the first were of godly intent and purpose devised, and yet at[r] length turned to vanity and superstition: Some entered into the Church by undiscreet devotion, and such a zeal as was without knowledge; and for because they were winked at in the beginning, they grew daily to more and more abuses, which not only for their unprofitableness, but also because they have much blinded the people, and obscured the glory of God, are worthy to be cut away, and clean rejected. Other there be, which although they have been devised by man, yet it is thought good to reserve them still, as well for a decent order in the Church (for the which they were first devised) as because they pertain to edification, whereunto all things done in the church (as the Apostle teacheth) ought to be referred. And although the keeping or omitting of a ceremony (in itself considered) is but a small thing: yet the wilful and contemptuous transgression, and breaking of a common order, and discipline, is no small offence before God. Let all things be done among you (saith Saint Paul) in a seemly and due order. The appointment of the which order pertaineth not to private men: Therefore no man ought to take in hand, nor presume to appoint or alter any public or common order in Christ's Church, except he be lawfully called and authorized thereunto. And whereas, in this our time, the minds of men be so diverse, that some think it a great matter

[r] In some copies, "at the."

of conscience to depart from a piece of the least of their ceremonies (they be so addicted to their old customs), and again on the other side, some be so new fangle that they would innovate all thing, and so do despise the old that nothing can like them, but that is new: It was thought expedient not so much to have respect how to please and satisfy either of these parties, as how to please God, and profit them both. And yet lest any man should be offended (whom good reason might satisfy), here be certain causes rendered why some of the accustomed ceremonies be put away, and some be retained and kept still.

Some are put away, because the great excess and multitude of them hath so increased in these latter days, that the burden of them was intolerable: whereof St. Augustine in his time complained, that they were grown to such a number, that the state of Christian people was in worse case (concerning that matter) than were the Jews. And he counselled that such yoke and burden should be taken away, as time would serve quietly to do it. But what would St. Augustine have said, if he had seen the ceremonies of late days used among us, whereunto the multitude used in his time was not to be compared? This our excessive multitude of ceremonies was so great, and many of them so dark, that they did more confound and darken, than declare and set forth Christ's benefits unto us. And besides this, Christ's Gospel is not a ceremonial law (as much of Moses' law was); but it is a religion to serve God, not in bondage of the figure or shadow, but in the freedom of spirit, being content only with those ceremonies which do serve to a decent order and godly discipline, and such as be apt to stir up the dull mind of man, to the remembrance of his duty to God, by some notable and special signification, whereby he might be edified.

¶ Furthermore, the most weighty cause of the abolishment of certain ceremonies was, that they were so far abused, partly by the superstitious blindness of the rude and unlearned, and partly by the unsatiable avarice of such as sought more their own lucre than the glory of God; that the abuses could not well be taken away, the thing remaining still. But now as concerning those persons, which peradventure will be offended for that some of the old ceremonies are retained still: if they consider, that without some ceremonies it is not possible to keep any order or quiet discipline in the church, they shall easily perceive just cause to reform their judgments. And if they think much that any of the old do remain, and would rather have all devised anew: then such men (granting some ceremonies convenient to be had), surely where the old may be well used, there they cannot reasonably reprove the old (only for their age) without bewraying of their own folly. For in such a case they ought rather to have reverence unto them for their antiquity, if they will declare themselves to be more studious of unity and concord, than of innovations and newfangleness, which (as much as may be with the true setting forth of Christ's religion) is always to be eschewed. Furthermore, such shall have no just cause with the ceremonies reserved to be offended: for as those be taken away which were most abused, and did burden men's consciences without any cause; so the other that remain are retained for a discipline and order, which (upon just causes) may be altered and changed, and therefore are not to be esteemed equal with God's law. And moreover they be neither dark nor dumb ceremonies, but are so set forth that every man may understand what they do mean, and to what use they do serve. So that it is not like that they, in time to come, should be abused as the other have been. And in these all our doings we condemn no other nations, nor prescribe any thing, but to our own people only. For we think it convenient that every country should use such ceremonies, as they shall think best to the setting forth of God's honour and glory, and to the reducing of the people to a most perfect and godly living, without error or superstition; and that they should put away other things, which from time to time they perceive to be most abused, as in men's ordinances it often chanceth diversely in diverse countries.

CERTAIN NOTES FOR THE MORE PLAIN EXPLICATION AND DECENT MINISTRATION OF THINGS CONTAINED IN THIS BOOK.

In the saying or singing of Matins and Evensong, Baptizing and Burying, the minister, in parish churches and chapels annexed to the same, shall use a Surplice. And in all Cathedral churches and Colleges, the Archdeacons, Deans, Provosts, Masters, Prebendaries, and Fellows, being graduates, may use in the quire, beside their Surplices, such hood as pertaineth to their several degrees, which they have taken in any university within this realm. But in all other places, every minister shall be at liberty to use any surplice or no. It is also seemly that graduates, when they do preach, shall use such hoods as pertaineth to their several degrees.

¶ *And whensoever the Bishop shall celebrate the holy communion in the church, or execute any other public ministration, he shall have upon him, beside his rochette, a Surplice or albe, and a cope or vestment, and also his pastoral staff in his hand, or else borne or holden by his chaplain.*

¶ *As touching kneeling, crossing, holding up of hands, knocking upon the breast, and other gestures, they may be used or left, as every man's devotion serveth, without blame.*

¶ *Also upon Christmas day, Easter day, the Ascension Day, Whit-Sunday, and the feast of the Trinity, may be used any part of holy scripture hereafter to be certainly limited and appointed, in the stead of the Litany.*

¶ If there be a sermon, or for other great cause, the Curate by his discretion may leave out the Litany, Gloria in Excelsis, the Creed, the Homily, and the Exhortation to the Communion.

FINIS.

Imprinted at London in Fletestrete, at the signe of the Sunne ouer against the conduyte, by EdVVarde VVhitchurche. The fourth daye of Maye [s], the yeare of our Lorde, 1549.

[In the more perfect copies the Prices are added thus.]

[t] The Kinges Maiestie, by the aduyse of his moste deare uncle the Lord Protector and other his highnes Counsell, streightly chargeth and commaundeth, that no maner of person do [u] sell this present booke unbounde, aboue the price of ii. shyllynges & ii.[x] pence the piece [y]. And the same bounde in paste or in boordes [z], not aboue the price of three [a] shyllynges and viii. pence the piece.

GOD SAUE THE KING.

---

[s] **In one ed.**, "7th day of March;" in another, "xvi day of June." The colophons in the books printed by Grafton run, "Imprinted at London the viii day of March, in the third yere of the reigne of our Soueraigne Lord Kyng Edward VI. by Richard Grafton, printer to his most royal Majestie." Also, "Excussum Londini in ædibus Richardi Graftoni Regii Impressoris Mense Junii M D XLIX."

[t] In some copies, "The King's Majesty," &c., *omitted*; in another, it is placed before the colophon.

[u] In some copies, "shall."   [x] In some copies. "six."

[y] In some copies, "the piece" *omitted*.

[z] In some copies, "covered with calves' leather;" in another, "in calves' leather."   [a] In some copies, "four shillings."

The forme
and maner of makyng and consecratyng of Archebishoppes Bishoppes Priestes and Deacons
M.D.XLIX.

This Ordinal was not printed as part of the first issues of the Prayer-Book of 1549, but as the colophons of some copies shew, it was intended to be bound up with copies of the Prayer-Book.

THE PREFACE.

It is evident unto all men, diligently reading holy scripture, and ancient authors, that from the Apostles' time there hath been these orders of Ministers in Christ's church: Bishops, Priests, and Deacons: which Offices were evermore had in such reverent estimation, that no man by his own private authority might presume to execute any of them, except he were first called, tried, examined, and known to have such qualities as were requisite for the same; and also, by public prayer, with imposition of hands, approved, and admitted thereunto. And therefore, to the intent these orders should be continued, and reverently used, and esteemed, in this Church of England, it is requisite, that no man (not being at this present Bishop, Priest, nor Deacon) shall execute any of them, except he be called, tried, examined, and admitted, according to the form hereafter following. And none shall be admitted a Deacon, except he be twenty-one years of age at the least. And every man which is to be admitted a Priest, shall be full twenty-four years old. And every man, which is to be consecrated a Bishop, shall be fully thirty years of age. And the Bishop knowing, either by himself, or by sufficient testimony, any person to be a man of virtuous conversation, and without crime, and after examination and trial, finding him learned in the Latin tongue, and sufficiently instructed in holy scripture, may, upon a Sunday or holyday, in the face of the church, admit him a Deacon, in such manner and form, as hereafter followeth.

THE FORM AND MANNER OF ORDERING OF DEACONS.

¶ *First, when the day appointed by the Bishop is come, there shall be an exhortation, declaring the duty and office of such as come to be admitted Ministers, how necessary such orders are in the church of Christ, and also, how the people ought to esteem them in their vocation.*

¶ *After the exhortation ended, the Archdeacon, or his deputy, shall present such as come to be admitted, to the Bishop; every one of them, that are presented, having upon him a plain Albe: and the Archdeacon, or his deputy, shall say these words.*

REVEREND Father in GOD, I present unto you these persons present, to be admitted Deacons.

¶ *The Bishop.* Take heed that the persons whom ye present unto us, be apt and meet, for their learning, and Godly conversation, to exercise their ministry duly, to the honour of God, and edifying of his Church.

The Archdeacon shall answer.

I have enquired of them, and also examined them, and think them so to be.

¶ *And then the Bishop shall say unto the people,*

BRETHREN, if there be any of you, who knoweth any impediment, or notable crime, in any of these persons presented to be ordered Deacons, for the which he ought not to be admitted to the same, let him come forth, in the name of God, and shew what the crime, or impediment is.

¶ *And if any great crime or impediment be objected, the Bishop shall surcease from ordering that person, until such time as the party accused shall try himself clear of that crime.*

Then the Bishop, commending such as shall be found meet to be ordered, to the prayers of the congregation, with the Clerks, and people present, shall say or sing the Litany as followeth.

The Litany and Suffrages.

O GOD the Father of heaven : have mercy upon us miserable sinners.

O God the Father of heaven : have mercy upon us miserable sinners.

O God the Son, Redeemer of the world : have mercy upon us miserable sinners.

O God the Son, Redeemer of the world : have mercy upon us miserable sinners.

O God the Holy Ghost, proceeding from the Father and the Son : have mercy upon us miserable sinners.

O God the Holy Ghost, proceeding from the Father and the Son : have mercy upon us miserable sinners.

O holy, blessed, and glorious Trinity, three persons and one God : have mercy upon us miserable sinners.

O holy, blessed, and glorious Trinity, three persons and one God : have mercy upon us miserable sinners.

Remember not, Lord, our offences, nor the offences of our forefathers, neither take thou vengeance of our sins : spare us, good Lord, spare thy people, whom thou hast redeemed with thy most precious blood, and be not angry with us for ever.

Spare us, good Lord.

From all evil and mischief, from sin, from the crafts

and assaults of the devil, from thy wrath, and from everlasting damnation.
Good Lord, deliver us.
From blindness of heart, from pride, vainglory, and hypocrisy, from envy, hatred, and malice, and all uncharitableness.
Good Lord, deliver us.
From fornication, and all deadly sin; and from all the deceits of the world, the flesh, and the devil.
Good Lord, deliver us.
From Lightning and Tempest, from Plague, Pestilence, and Famine, from Battle and murther, and from sudden death.
Good Lord, deliver us.
From all sedition and privy conspiracy, from the tyranny of the Bishop of Rome, and all his detestable enormities, from all false doctrine and heresy, from hardness of heart, and contempt of thy word and commandment.
Good Lord, deliver us.
By the mystery of thy holy incarnation, by thy holy nativity and Circumcision, by thy baptism, fasting, and temptation.
Good Lord, deliver us.
By thine agony and bloody sweat, by thy Cross and passion, by thy precious death and burial, by thy glorious resurrection and ascension, by the coming of the Holy Ghost.
Good Lord, deliver us.
In all time of our tribulation, in all time of our wealth, in the hour of death, in the day of judgment.
Good Lord, deliver us.
We sinners do beseech thee to hear us (O Lord God), and that it may please thee to rule and govern thy holy church universal in the right way.
We beseech thee to hear us, good Lord.
That it may please thee, to keep EDWARD the VI. thy servant, our King and governor.
We beseech thee to hear us, good Lord.

That it may please thee, to rule his heart in thy faith, fear and love, that he may always have affiance in thee, and ever seek thy honour and glory.
We beseech thee to hear us, good Lord.

That it may please thee to be his defender and keeper, giving him the victory over all his enemies.
We beseech thee to hear us, good Lord.

That it may please thee, to illuminate all Bishops, Pastors, and ministers of the church, with true knowledge, and understanding of thy word, and that both by their preaching and living they may set it forth, and shew it accordingly.
We beseech thee to hear us, good Lord.

That it may please thee, to bless these men, and send thy grace upon them, that they may duly execute the office, now to be committed unto them, to the edifying of thy Church, and to thy honour, praise, and glory.
We beseech thee to hear us, good Lord.

That it may please thee to endue the lords of the council, and all the nobility, with grace, wisdom, and understanding.
We beseech thee to hear us, good Lord.

That it may please thee, to bless and keep the Magistrates, giving them grace to execute justice, and to maintain truth.
We beseech thee to hear us, good Lord.

That it may please thee, to bless and keep all thy people.
We beseech thee to hear us, good Lord.

That it may please thee, to give to all nations unity, peace, and concord.
We beseech thee to hear us, good Lord.

That it may please thee, to give us an heart, to love and dread thee, and diligently to live after thy commandments.
We beseech thee to hear us, good Lord.

That it may please thee, to give all thy people

The Ordering of Deacons.

increase of grace, to hear meekly thy word, and to receive it with pure affection, and to bring forth the fruits of the Spirit.

We beseech thee to hear us, good Lord.

That it may please thee, to bring into the way of truth all such as have erred and are deceived.

We beseech thee to hear us, good Lord.

That it may please thee, to strengthen such as do stand, and to comfort and help the weak-hearted, and to raise them up that fall, and finally to beat down Sathan under our feet.

We beseech thee to hear us, good Lord.

That it may please thee, to succour, help and comfort, all that be in danger, necessity and tribulation.

We beseech thee to hear us, good Lord.

That it may please thee, to preserve all that travel by land, or by water, all women labouring of child, all sick persons, and young children, and to shew thy pity upon all prisoners and captives.

We beseech thee to hear us, good Lord.

That it may please thee, to defend and provide for the fatherless children and widows, and all that be desolate and oppressed.

We beseech thee to hear us, good Lord.

That it may please thee, to have mercy upon all men.

We beseech thee to hear us, good Lord.

That it may please thee, to forgive our enemies, persecutors, and slanderers, and to turn their hearts.

We beseech thee to hear us, good Lord.

That it may please thee, to give and preserve to our use the kindly fruits of the earth, so as in due time we may enjoy them.

We beseech thee to hear us, good Lord.

That it may please thee, to give us true repentance, to forgive us all our sins, negligences, and ignorances,

and to endue us with the grace of thy holy Spirit to amend our lives, according to thy holy word.
We beseech thee to hear us, good Lord.

Son of GOD : we beseech thee to hear us.
Son of God : we beseech thee to hear us.

O Lamb of God, that takest away the sins of the world.
Grant us thy peace.

O Lamb of God, that takest away the sins of the world.
Have mercy upon us.

O Christ, hear us.
O Christ, hear us.

Lord, have mercy upon us.
Lord, have mercy upon us.

Christ, have mercy upon us.
Christ, have mercy upon us.

Lord, have mercy upon us.
Lord, have mercy upon us.

Our Father, which art in heaven,
With the residue of the Pater Noster.

And lead us not into temptation.
But deliver us from evil.

The Versicle. O Lord, deal not with us after our sins.

The Answer. Neither reward us after our iniquities.

Let us pray.

O GOD merciful Father, that despisest not the sighing of a contrite heart, nor the desire of such as be sorrowful, mercifully assist our prayers that we make before thee, in all our troubles and adversities, whensoever they oppress us : and graciously hear us, that those evils, which the craft and subtilty of the Devil, or man, worketh against us, be brought to nought, and by the providence of thy goodness they may be dispersed, that we thy servants, being hurt by no persecutions, may evermore give thanks unto thee, in thy holy Church : Through Jesu Christ our Lord.

O Lord, arise, help us, and deliver us, for thy name's sake.

O GOD, we have heard with our ears, and our fathers have declared unto us, the noble works, that thou didst in their days, and in the old time before them.

O Lord, arise, help us, and deliver us, for thine honour.

Glory be to the Father, the Son, and to the Holy Ghost : as it was in the beginning, is now, and ever shall be, world without end. Amen.

From our enemies defend us, O Christ.

Graciously look upon our afflictions.

Pitifully behold the dolor of our heart.

Mercifully forgive the sins of thy people.

Favourably with mercy hear our prayers.

O Son of David, have mercy upon us.

Both now and ever vouchsafe to hear us, O Christ.

Graciously hear us, O Christ.

Graciously hear us, O Lord Christ.

¶ *The Versicle.* O Lord, let thy mercy be shewed upon us.

The Answer. As we do put our trust in thee.

¶ Let us pray.

WE humbly beseech thee, O Father, mercifully to look upon our infirmities, and for the glory of thy name's sake, turn from us all those evils, that we most righteously have deserved : And grant that in all our troubles we may put our whole trust and confidence in thy mercy, and evermore serve thee, in pureness of living, to thy honour and glory, through our only mediator and advocate Jesus Christ our Lord. Amen.

ALMIGHTY God, which hast given us grace at this time with one accord to make our supplications unto thee, and dost promise, that when two or three be gathered in thy name, thou wilt grant their requests: fulfil now, O Lord, the desires and petitions of thy servants, as may be most expedient for them, granting us in this world knowledge of thy truth, and in the world to come life everlasting. Amen.

ALMIGHTY God, which by thy divine providence hast appointed diverse Orders of ministers in the church, and didst inspire thine holy Apostles to choose unto this Order of Deacons thy first Martyr saint Stephin, with other: mercifully behold these thy servants, now called to the like Office and ministration; replenish them so with the truth of thy doctrine, and innocency of life, that, both by word and good example, they may faithfully serve thee in this Office, to the glory of thy name, and profit of the congregation, through the merits of our Saviour Jesu Christ, who liveth and reigneth with thee, and the Holy Ghost, now and ever. Amen.

Then shall be sung or said, the Communion of the day, saving the Epistle shall be read out of Timothy, as followeth.

LIKEWISE must the ministers be honest, not double-tongued, nor given unto much wine, neither greedy of filthy lucre, but holding the mystery of the faith, with a pure conscience. And let them first be proved, and then let them minister so that no man be able to reprove them. Even so must their wives be honest, not evil speakers, but sober, and faithful in all things. Let the Deacons be the husbands of one wife, and such as rule their children well, and their own households. For they that minister well get themselves a good degree, and a great liberty in the faith which is in Christ Jesu.

These things write I unto thee trusting to come shortly unto thee; but and if I tarry long, that then thou mayest yet have knowledge, how thou oughtest to behave thyself in the house of God, which is the congregation of the living God, the pillar and ground of truth. And without doubt great is that mystery of godliness. God was shewed in the flesh, was justified in the spirit, was seen among the angels, was preached unto the Gentiles, was believed on in the world, and received up in glory.

Or else this, out of the sixth of the Acts.

THEN the twelve called the multitude of the disciples together, and said : It is not meet that we should leave the Word of God, and serve tables. Wherefore, brethren, look ye out among you seven men of honest report, and full of the holy Ghost and wisdom, to whom we may commit this business. But we will give ourselves continually to prayer, and to the administration of the Word. And that saying pleased the whole multitude. And they chose Stephen, a man full of faith, and full of the holy Ghost, and Philip, and Prochorus, and Nicanor, and Timon, and Permenas, and Nicolas a convert of Antioch. These they set before the Apostles : and, when they had prayed, they laid their hands on them. And the Word of God increased, and the number of the disciples multiplied in Jerusalem greatly, and a great company of the Priests, were obedient unto the faith.

¶ *And before the Gospel, the Bishop sitting in a Chair, shall cause the Oath of the King's Supremacy, and against the usurped power and authority of the Bishop of Rome, to be ministered unto every of them, that are to be ordered.*

¶ *The Oath of the* King's Supremacy.

I FROM henceforth shall utterly renounce, refuse, relinquish, and forsake the Bishop of Rome, and his authority, power, and jurisdiction. And I shall never consent nor agree, that the bishop of Rome shall practise, exercise, or have, any manner of authority, jurisdiction, or power within this realm, or any other the king's dominions, but shall resist the same at all times, to the uttermost of my power. And I from henceforth will accept, repute, and take the King's Majesty to be the only supreme head in earth, of the church of England: And to my cunning, wit, and uttermost of my power, without guile, fraud, or other undue mean, I will observe, keep, maintain and defend, the whole effects and contents of all and singular acts and statutes made, and to be made within this realm, in derogation, extirpation, and extinguishment of the Bishop of Rome, and his authority, and all other acts and statutes, made or to be made, in reformation and corroboration of the King's power, of the supreme head in earth, of the church of England: and this I will do against all manner of persons, of what estate, dignity or degree, or condition they be, and in no wise do nor attempt, nor to my power suffer to be done or attempted, directly, or indirectly, any thing or things, privily or apertly, to the let, hinderance, damage, or derogation thereof, or any part thereof, by any manner of means, or for any manner of pretence. And in case any other be made, or hath been made, by me, to any person or persons, in maintenance, defence, or favour of the Bishop of Rome, or his authority, jurisdiction, or power, I repute the same as vain and annihilate, so help me GOD, all saints and the holy Evangelist.

Then shall the Bishop examine every one of them, that are to be ordered, in the presence of the people, after this manner following.

Do you trust that you are inwardly moved by the Holy Ghost to take upon you this Office and ministration, to serve GOD, for the promoting of his glory, and the edifying of his people?

Answer. I trust so.

The Bishop. Do ye think, that ye truly be called, according to the will of our Lord Jesus Christ, and the due order of this realm to the ministry of the church?

Answer. I think so.

The Bishop. Do ye unfeignedly believe all the Canonical scriptures, of the old and new Testament?

Answer. I do believe.

The Bishop. Will you diligently read the same unto the people assembled in the church where you shall be appointed to serve?

Answer. I will.

The Bishop. It pertaineth to the office of a Deacon to assist the Priest in divine service, and specially when he ministereth the holy Communion, and help him in the distribution thereof, and to read holy scriptures and Homilies in the congregation, and instruct the youth in the Catechism, and also to baptize and preach if he be commanded by the Bishop. And furthermore, it is his office to search for the sick, poor, and impotent people of the parish, and to intimate their estates, names, and places where they dwell to the Curate, that by his exhortation they may be relieved by the parish or other convenient alms: will you do this gladly and willingly?

Answer. I will so do by the help of God.

The Bishop. Will you apply all your diligence to frame and fashion your own lives, and the lives of all your family according to the doctrine of Christ, and to make both yourselves and them, as much as in you lieth, wholesome examples of the flock of Christ?

Answer. I will so do, the Lord being my helper.

The Bishop. Will you reverently obey your ordinary and other chief Ministers of the Church, and them to whom the government and charge is committed over you, following with a glad mind and will their godly admonitions?

Answer. I will thus endeavour myself, the Lord being my helper.

¶ *Then the Bishop laying his hands severally upon the head of every one of them, shall say.*

Take thou authority to execute the office of a Deacon in the Church of God committed unto thee: in the name of the Father, the Son, and the Holy Ghost. Amen.

Then shall the Bishop deliver to every one of them the new Testament, saying.

Take thou authority to read the Gospel in the Church of God, and to preach the same, if thou be thereunto ordinarily commanded.

Then one of them, appointed by the Bishop, putting on a tunicle, shall read the Gospel of that day.

Then shall the Bishop proceed to the Communion, and all that be ordered, shall tarry and receive the holy communion the same day with the Bishop.

The Communion ended, after the last collect and immediately before the benediction, shall be said this Collect following.

ALMIGHTY God, giver of all good things, which of thy great goodness hast vouchsafed to accept and take these thy servants unto the office of Deacons in thy church: make them, we beseech thee, O Lord, to be modest, humble, and constant in their ministration, and to have a ready will to observe all spiritual discipline, that they having always the testimony of a good conscience, and continuing ever stable and strong in thy Son Christ, may so well use themselves in this inferior office, that they may be found worthy to be called unto the higher ministries in thy Church, through the same thy Son our Saviour Christ, to whom be glory and honour world without end. Amen.

¶ *And here it must be shewed unto the Deacon, that he must continue in that office of a Deacon the space of a whole year at the least (except for reasonable causes it be otherwise seen to his ordinary) to the intent he may be perfect, and well expert in the things appertaining to the Ecclesiastical administration, in executing whereof if he be found faithful and diligent, he may be admitted by his diocesan to the order of Priesthood.*

THE FORM

OF

ORDERING OF PRIESTS.

When the exhortation is ended, then shall be sung, for the Introit to the Communion, this Psalm.
Expectans expectavi Dominum. Psalm xl.

Or else this Psalm.
Memento Domine David. Psalm cxxxii.

Or else this Psalm.
Laudate nomen Domini. Psalm cxxxv.

Then shall be read for the Epistle this out of the xx. Chapter of the Acts of the Apostles.

FROM Mileto Paul sent messengers to Ephesus, and called the elders of the congregation, which when they were come to him, he said unto them, Ye know, that from the first day that I came into Asia, after what manner I have been with you at all seasons, serving the Lord with all humbleness of mind, and with many tears and temptations which happened unto me by the layings await of the Jews; because I would keep back nothing that was profitable unto you, but to shew you, and teach you openly throughout every house: witnessing both to the Jews, and also to the Greeks, the repentance that is towards God, and the faith which is toward our Lord Jesus Christ. And now behold, I go bound in the spirit unto Jerusalem, not knowing the things that shall come on me there; but that the Holy Ghost witnesseth in every city, saying, that bonds and trouble abide me. But none of these things move me, neither is my life dear unto myself, that I might fulfil my course with joy, and the ministration of the word which I have received of the Lord Jesu, to testify the Gospel of the grace of God. And now behold, I am sure that henceforth ye all, through whom I have gone preaching the kingdom of God, shall see my face no more. Wherefore I take you to record this day, that I am pure from the blood of all men. For I have spared no labour, but have shewed you all the counsel of God. Take heed therefore unto yourselves, and to all the flock amongst whom the Holy Ghost hath made you Overseers, to rule the congregation of God, which he hath purchased with his blood. For I am sure of this, that after my departing shall grievous wolves enter in among you, not sparing the flock. Moreover of your own selves shall men arise speaking perverse things, to draw disciples after them. Therefore awake and remember, that by the space of three years, I ceased not to warn every one of you night and day with tears. And now, brethren, I commend you to God, and to the word of his grace, which is able to build further, and to give you an inheritance among all them which are sanctified. I have desired no man's silver, gold, or vesture; Yea, you know yourselves, that these hands have ministered unto my necessities, and to them that were with me. I have shewed you all things, how that so labouring ye ought to receive the weak; and to remember the words of the Lord Jesu, how that he said, It is more blessed to give than to receive.

Or else this third Chapter of the first Epistle to Timothy.

THIS is a true saying, If any man desire the Office of a Bishop, he desireth an honest work. A Bishop therefore must be blameless, the husband of one wife, vigilant, sober, discreet, a keeper of hospitality, apt to teach; not given to overmuch wine, no fighter, not greedy of filthy lucre, but gentle, abhorring fighting, abhorring covetousness; one that ruleth well his own house, one that hath children in subjection with all reverence. (For if a man cannot rule his own house, how shall he care for the congregation of God?) He may not be a young scholar, lest he swell and fall into the judgement of the evil speaker. He must also have a good report of them which are without; lest he fall into rebuke and snare of the evil speaker.

Likewise must the ministers be honest, not double-tongued, not given unto much wine, neither greedy of filthy lucre; but holding the mystery of the faith with a pure conscience; and let them first be proved, and then let them minister so that no man be able to reprove them.

Even so must their wives be honest; not evil-speakers, but sober and faithful in all things. Let the deacons be the husbands of one wife, and such as rule their children well and their own households, for they that minister well get themselves a good degree and great liberty in the faith which is in Christ Jesu.

These things write I unto thee, trusting to come shortly unto thee, but, and if I tarry long, that then thou mayest have yet knowledge how thou oughtest to behave thy self in the house of God, which is the congregation of the living God, the Pillar and ground of truth. And without doubt, great is that mystery of Godliness. God was shewed in the flesh, was Justified in the Spirit, was seen among the Angels, was preached unto the Gentiles, was believed on in the world, and received up in glory.

After this shall be read for the Gospel a piece of the last Chapter of Matthew, as followeth.

JESUS came and spake unto them, saying: All power is given unto me in heaven and in earth. Go ye therefore and teach all nations, baptizing them In the name of the father, and of the son, and of the holy ghost. Teaching them to observe all things, whatsoever I have commanded you. And lo, I am with you alway, even until the end of the world.

Or else this that followeth, of the x. Chapter of John.

VERILY, verily I say unto you, He that entereth not in by the door into the sheep-fold, but climbeth up some other way, the same is a thief and a murtherer. But he that entereth in by the door is the Shepherd of the sheep. To him the porter openeth, and the sheep heareth his voice, and he calleth his own sheep by name, and leadeth them out. And when he hath sent forth his own sheep he goeth before them, and the sheep follow him, for they know his voice. A stranger will they not follow, but will flee from him; for they know not the voice of strangers. This Proverb spake Jesus unto them, but they understood not what things they were which he spake unto them. Then said Jesus unto them again, Verily, verily I say unto you, I am the door of the sheep. All (even as many as come before me) are thieves and murtherers: but the sheep did not hear them. I am the door, by me if any man enter in, he shall be safe, and go in and out, and find pasture. A thief cometh not but for to steal, kill, and to destroy. I am come that they might have life, and that they might have it more abundantly. I am the good Shepherd: a good Shepherd giveth his life for the sheep. An hired servant, and he which is not the Shepherd (neither the sheep are his own) seeth the wolf coming, and leaveth the sheep, and fleeth, and the wolf catcheth and scattereth the sheep. The hired servant fleeth, because he is an hired servant, and careth not for the sheep. I am the good Shepherd and know my sheep, and am known of mine. As my Father knoweth me, even so know I also my Father. And I give my life for the sheep. And other sheep I have, which are not of this fold. Them also must I bring, and they shall hear my voice, and there shall be one fold, and one Shepherd.

The Ordering of Priests. 191

Or else this, of the xx. chapter of John.

THE same day at night, which was the first day of the Sabboths, when the doors were shut (where the disciples were assembled together for fear of the Jews) came Jesus and stood in the midst, and saith unto them, Peace be unto you. And when he had so said, he shewed unto them his hands and his side. Then were the disciples glad, when they saw the Lord. Then said Jesus unto them again, Peace be unto you. As my Father sent me, even so send I you also. And when he had said these words, he breathed on them, and said unto them, Receive ye the holy ghost: whosesoever sins ye remit, they are remitted unto them: and whosesoever sins ye retain, they are retained.

When the Gospel is ended, then shall be said or sung.

COME Holy Ghost eternal God, proceeding from above,
Both from the Father and the Son, the God of peace and love:
Visit our minds, and into us thy heavenly grace inspire,
That in all truth and Godliness we may have true desire.

Thou art the very comforter, in all woe and distress,
The heavenly gift of God most high, which no tongue can express,
The fountain and the lively spring of joy celestial,
The fire so bright, the love so clear, and unction spiritual.

Thou in thy gifts art manifold, whereby Christ's Church doth stand,
In faithful hearts writing thy law, the finger of God's hand:

According to thy promise made, thou givest speech of grace,
That through thy help, the praise of God may sound in every place.

O Holy Ghost, into our wits send down thy heavenly light,
Kindle our hearts with fervent love, to serve God day and night,
Strength and stablish all our weakness, so feeble and so frail,
That neither flesh, the world, nor devil, against us do prevail.

Put back our enemy far from us, and grant us to obtain
Peace in our hearts with God and man, without grudge or disdain.
And grant, O Lord, that thou being our leader and our guide,
We may eschew the snares of sin, and from thee never slide.

To us such plenty of thy grace, good Lord, grant, we thee pray,
That thou Lord mayest be our comfort, at the last dreadful day.
Of all strife and dissension, O Lord, dissolve the bands,
And make the knots of peace and love throughout all Christian lands.

Grant us, O Lord, through thee to know the Father most of might,
That of his dear beloved Son we may attain the sight:
And that with perfit faith also we may acknowledge thee,
The Spirit of them both, alway one God in persons three.

THE ORDERING OF PRIESTS. 193

Laud and praise be to the Father, and to the Son equal,
And to the Holy Spirit also, one God coeternal:
And pray we that the only Son vouchsafe his Spirit to send
To all that do profess his name, unto the world's end. Amen.

And then the Archdeacon shall present unto the Bishop all them that shall receive the order of Priesthood that day, every of them having upon him a plain Albe: The Archdeacon saying.

REVEREND father in God, I present unto you these persons present, to be admitted to the Order of Priesthood, *cum interrogatione et responsione, ut in Ordine Diaconatus.*

And then the Bishop shall say to the people.

GOOD people, these be they whom we purpose, God willing, to receive this day unto the holy office of Priesthood. For after due examination, we find not the contrary, but that they be lawfully called to their function and ministry, and that they be persons meet for the same. But yet if there be any of you, which knoweth any impediment, or notable crime in any of them, for the which he ought not to be received to this holy ministry, now in the name of God declare the same.

¶ *And if any great crime or impediment be objected, &c.* ut supra in Ordine Diaconatus usque ad finem Litaniæ cum hac Collecta.

ALMIGHTY God, giver of all good things, which by thy Holy Spirit hast appointed diverse orders of Ministers in thy church: mercifully behold these thy servants, now called to the Office of Priesthood, and replenish them so with the truth of thy doctrine, and innocency of life, that both by word and good example they may faithfully serve thee in this office, to the glory of thy name, and profit of the congregation, through the merits of our Saviour Jesu Christ, who liveth and reigneth, with thee and the Holy Ghost, world without end. Amen.

¶ *Then the Bishop shall minister unto every of them the oath, concerning the King's Supremacy, as it is set out in the Order of Deacons. And that done, he shall say unto them, which are appointed to receive the said Office, as hereafter followeth.*

YOU have heard, brethren, as well in your private examination, as in the exhortation, and in the holy lessons taken out of the Gospel, and of the writings of the Apostles, of what dignity, and of how great importance this office is, (whereunto ye be called). And now we exhort you, in the name of our Lord Jesus Christ, to have in remembrance, into how high a dignity, and to how chargeable an office ye be called, that is to say, to be the Messengers, the Watchmen, the Pastors, and the Stewards of the Lord, to teach, to premonish, to feed, and provide for the Lord's family: to seek for Christ's Sheep, that be dispersed abroad, and for his children, which be in the midst of this naughty world, to be saved through Christ for ever. Have always therefore printed in your remembrance, how great a treasure is committed to your charge: for they be the Sheep of Christ, which he bought with his death, and for whom he shed his blood. The Church and congregation, whom you must serve, is his spouse and his body. And if it shall chance the same Church, or any member thereof, to take any hurt or hinderance by reason of your negligence, ye know the greatness of the fault, and also of the horrible punishment which will ensue. Wherefore, consider with yourselves the end of your ministry, towards the children of God, toward the spouse and body of Christ, and see that ye never cease your labour, your care and diligence, until you have done all that lieth in you, according to your bounden duty, to bring all such as are, or shall be committed to your charge, unto that agreement in faith, and knowledge of God, and to that ripeness, and perfectness of age in Christ, that there be no place left among them, either for error in religion, or for viciousness in life.

Then forasmuch as your office is both of so great excellency, and of so great difficulty, ye see with how great care and study ye ought to apply yourselves, as well that you may shew yourselves kind to that Lord, who hath placed you in so high a dignity, as also to beware, that neither you yourselves offend, neither be occasion that other offend. Howbeit ye cannot have a mind and a will thereto of yourselves, for that power and ability is given of God alone. Therefore ye see how ye ought and have need, earnestly to pray for his Holy Spirit. And seeing that ye cannot, by any other means, compass the doing of so weighty a work, pertaining to the salvation of man, but with doctrine and exhortation, taken out of holy Scripture and with a life agreeable unto the same, ye perceive how studious ye ought to be in reading and learning the holy scriptures, and in framing the manners, both of yourselves, and of them that specially pertain unto you, according to the rule of the same scriptures. And for this selfsame cause, ye see how you ought to forsake and set aside (as much as you may) all worldly cares and studies.

We have a good hope, that you have well weighed and pondered these things with yourselves, long before this time, and that you have clearly determined, by God's grace, to give yourselves wholly to this vocation, whereunto it hath pleased God to call you, so that (as much as lieth in you) you apply yourselves wholly to this one thing, and draw all your cares and studies this way, and to this end. And that you will continually pray for the heavenly assistance of the Holy Ghost, from God the Father, by the mediation of our only Mediator and Saviour Jesus Christ, that by daily reading and weighing of the scriptures ye may wax riper and stronger in your Ministry: and that ye may so endeavour yourselves, from time to time, to sanctify the lives of you and yours, and to fashion them, after the rule and doctrine of Christ, and that ye may be wholesome and godly examples and patterns, for the rest of the congregation to follow: and that this present congregation of Christ, here assembled, may also understand your minds and wills, in these things.

¶ And that this your promise shall more move you to do your duties, ye shall answer plainly to these things, which we in the name of the Congregation shall demand of you, touching the same.

Do you think in your heart, that you be truly called, according to the will of our Lord Jesus Christ, and the order of this Church of England, to the ministry of Priesthood?

Answer. I think it.

The Bishop. Be you persuaded that the holy scriptures contain sufficiently all doctrine, required of necessity for eternal salvation, through faith in Jesu Christ? And are you determined with the said scriptures to instruct the people committed to your charge, and to teach nothing, as required of necessity to eternal salvation, but that you shall be persuaded, may be concluded, and proved by the scripture?

Answer. I am so persuaded, and have so determined by God's grace.

The Bishop. Will you then give your faithful diligence always, so to minister the doctrine, and Sacraments, and the discipline of Christ, as the Lord hath commanded, and as this realm hath received the same, according to the commandments of God, so that ye may teach the people committed to your cure and charge with all diligence to keep and observe the same?

Answer. I will so do, by the help of the Lord.

The Bishop. Will you be ready with all faithful diligence to banish and drive away all erroneous and strange doctrines contrary to God's word, and to use both public and private monitions and exhortations, as well to the sick as to the whole, within your cures, as need shall require and occasion be given?

Answer. I will, the Lord being my helper.

The Bishop. Will you be diligent in prayers and in reading of the holy scriptures, and in such studies as help to the knowledge of the same, laying aside the study of the world and the flesh?

Answer. I will endeavour myself so to do, the Lord being my helper.

The Bishop. Will you be diligent to frame and fashion your own selves and your families according to the doctrine of Christ, and to make both yourselves and them (as much as in you lieth) wholesome examples and spectacles to the flock of Christ?

Answer. I will so apply myself, the Lord being my helper.

The Bishop. Will you maintain and set forwards (as much as lieth in you) quietness, peace, and love amongst all Christian people, and specially amongst them that are or shall be committed to your charge?

Answer. I will so do, the Lord being my helper.

The Bishop. Will you reverently obey your ordinary, and other chief ministers, unto whom the government and charge is committed over you, following with a glad mind and will their godly admonition, and submitting yourselves to their godly judgments?

Answer. I will so do, the Lord being my helper.

¶ *Then shall the Bishop say,*

ALMIGHTY God, who hath given you this will to do all these things, grant also unto you strength and power to perform the same, that he may accomplish his work which he hath begun in you, until the time he shall come at the latter day to judge the quick and the dead.

¶ *After this the congregation shall be desired secretly in their prayers to make humble supplications to God for the foresaid things, for the which prayers there shall be a certain space kept in silence.*

That done, the Bishop shall pray in this wise.
The Lord be with you.
Answer. And with thy spirit.

¶ Let us pray.

ALMIGHTY God and heavenly Father, which of thy infinite love and goodness towards us, hast given to us thy only and most dear beloved Son Jesus Christ, to be our redeemer and author of everlasting life: who after he had made perfect our redemption by his death, and was ascended into heaven, sent abroad into the world his Apostles, Prophets, Evangelists, Doctors, and Pastors, by whose labour and ministry he gathered together a great flock in all the parts of the world, to set forth the eternal praise of thy holy name: For these so great benefits of thy eternal goodness, and for that thou hast vouchsafed to call these thy servants here present to the same office and ministry of the salvation of mankind, we render unto thee most hearty thanks, we worship and praise thee; and we humbly beseech thee by the same thy Son, to grant unto all us which either here or elsewhere call upon thy name, that we may shew ourselves thankful to thee for these and all other thy benefits, and that we may daily increase and go forwards in the knowledge and faith of thee, and thy Son, by the Holy Spirit. So that as well by these thy ministers, as by them to whom they shall be appointed ministers, thy holy name may be always glorified, and thy blessed

THE ORDERING OF PRIESTS. 199

kingdom enlarged: through the same thy Son our Lord Jesus Christ, which liveth and reigneth with thee in the unity of the same Holy Spirit world without end. Amen.

¶ *When this prayer is done, the Bishop with the Priests present shall lay their hands severally upon the head of every one that receiveth orders. The receivers humbly kneeling upon their knees, and the Bishop saying:*

RECEIVE the Holy Ghost: whose sins thou dost forgive, they are forgiven: and whose sins thou dost retain, they are retained: and be thou a faithful dispenser of the word of God, and of his holy sacraments. In the name of the Father, and of the Son, and of the Holy Ghost. Amen.

The Bishop shall deliver to every one of them the Bible in the one hand, and the Chalice or cup with the bread, in the other hand, and say.

TAKE thou authority to preach the word of God, and to minister the holy Sacraments in this Congregation.

¶ *When this is done, the Congregation shall sing the Creed, and also they shall go to the Communion, which all they that receive orders shall take together, and remain in the same place where the hands were laid upon them, until such time as they have received the Communion.*

¶ *The Communion being done, after the last Collect, and immediately before the benediction, shall be said this Collect:*

MOST merciful Father, we beseech thee, so to send upon these thy Servants thy heavenly blessing, that they may be clad about with all justice, and that thy word spoken by their mouths may have such success, that it may never be spoken in vain. Grant also that we may have grace to hear and receive the same as thy most holy word and the mean of our salvation, that in all our words and deeds we may seek thy glory and the increase of thy kingdom, through Jesus Christ our Lord. Amen.

¶ *If the orders of Deacon and Priesthood be given both upon one day, then shall the Psalm for the Introit and other things at the holy Communion be used as they are appointed at the ordering of Priests. Saving that for the Epistle, the whole iii. chapter of the first to Timothy shall be read, as it is set out before in the order of Priests. And immediately after the Epistle, the Deacons shall be ordered. And it shall suffice the Litany to be said once.*

THE FORM OF CONSECRATING

OF AN

ARCHBISHOP OR BISHOP.

The Psalm for the Introit at the Communion, as at the Ordering of Priests.

The Epistle.

THIS is a true saying, If a man desire the office of a Bishop, he desireth an honest work. A Bishop therefore must be blameless, the husband of one wife, diligent, sober, discreet, a keeper of hospitality, apt to teach, not given to overmuch wine, no fighter, not greedy of filthy lucre, but gentle, abhorring fighting, abhorring covetousness, one that ruleth well his own house; one that hath children in subjection with all reverence. For if a man cannot rule his own house, how shall he care for the congregation of God? he may not be a young scholar, lest he swell, and fall into the judgment of the evil speaker. He must also have a good report of them which are without, lest he fall into rebuke and snare of the evil speaker. 1 Tim. iii.

The Gospel.

JESUS said to Simon Peter, Simon Johanna, lovest thou me more than these? He said unto him, Yea, Lord, thou knowest that I love thee. He said unto him, Feed my lambs. He said to him again the second time: Simon Johanna, lovest thou me? He said unto him, Yea, Lord, thou knowest that I love thee. He said unto him, Feed my sheep. He said unto him the third time, Simon Johanna, lovest thou me? Peter was sorry because he said unto him the third time, Lovest thou me? and he said unto him: Lord, thou knowest all things, John xxi.

thou knowest that I love thee. Jesus said unto him, Feed my sheep.

¶ *Or else out of the x. Chapter of John, as before in the order of Priests.*

¶ *After the Gospel and Credo ended, first the elected Bishop, having upon him a surplice and a cope, shall be presented by two Bishops (being also in surplices and copes, and having their pastoral staves in their hands) unto the Archbishop of the Province, or to some other Bishop appointed by his commission: the Bishops that present, saying:*

MOST reverend Father in God, we present unto you this godly and well learned man to be consecrated Bishop.

¶ *And then the King's mandate to the Archbishop for the consecration shall be read. And the oath touching the knowledging of the King's supremacy shall be ministered to the person elected, as it is set out in the order of Deacons. And then shall be ministered also the Oath of due obedience unto the Archbishop as followeth.*

¶ THE OATH OF DUE OBEdience to the Archbishop.

IN the name of GOD, Amen. I, N. chosen Bishop of the church and see of N. do profess and promise all due reverence and obedience to the Archbishop and to the Metropolitical church of N. and to their successors, so help me God and his holy Gospel.

¶ *Then the Archbishop shall move the congregation present to pray, saying thus to them.*

BRETHREN, it is written in the Gospel of Saint Luke, that our Saviour Christ continued the whole night in prayer or ever that he did choose and send forth his xii. Apostles. It is written also in the Acts of the Apostles, that the disciples which were at Antioch did fast and pray or ever they laid hands upon or sent forth Paul and Barnabas. Let us therefore, following the example of our Saviour Christ and his Apostles, first fall to prayer or that we admit and send forth this person presented unto us, to the work whereunto we trust the Holy Ghost hath called him.

¶ *And then shall be said the Litany as afore in the order of Deacons. And after this place: That it may please thee to illuminate all Bishops &c. he shall say.*

THAT it may please thee to bless this our brother elected, and to send thy grace upon him, that he may duly execute the office whereunto he is called, to the edifying of thy church, and to the honour, praise and glory of thy name.
Answer. We beseech thee to hear us, good Lord.

Concluding the Litany in the end with this prayer:

ALMIGHTY God, giver of all good things, which by thy Holy Spirit hast appointed divers orders of Ministers in thy Church: mercifully behold this thy servant now called to the work and ministry of a Bishop, and replenish him so with the truth of thy doctrine and innocency of life, that both by word and deed he may faithfully serve thee in this office, to the glory of thy name, and profit of thy congregation: through the merits of our Saviour Jesu Christ, who liveth and reigneth with thee and the Holy Ghost, world without end. Amen.

Then the Archbishop sitting in a chair, shall say this to him that is to be consecrated.

BROTHER, forasmuch as holy Scripture and the old Canons commandeth that we should not be hasty in laying on hands and admitting of any person to the government of the congregation of Christ, which he hath purchased with no less price than the effusion of his own blood, afore that I admit you to this administration whereunto ye are called, I will examine you in certain articles, to the end the Congregation present may have a trial and bear witness how ye be minded to behave yourself in the church of God.

Are you persuaded that you be truly called to this ministration according to the will of our Lord Jesus Christ and the order of this realm?

Answer. I am so persuaded.

The Archbishop. Are you persuaded that the holy Scriptures contain sufficiently all doctrine required of necessity for eternal salvation through the faith in Jesu Christ? And are you determined with the same holy Scriptures to instruct the people committed to your charge, and to teach or maintain nothing, as required of necessity to eternal salvation, but that you shall be persuaded may be concluded and proved by the same?

Answer. I am so persuaded and determined by God's grace.

The Archbishop. Will you then faithfully exercise yourself in the said holy Scriptures, and call upon God by prayer for the true understanding of the same, so as ye may be able by them to teach and exhort with wholesome doctrine, and to withstand and convince the gainsayers?

Answer. I will so do, by the help of God.

The Archbishop. Be you ready with all faithful diligence to banish and drive away all erroneous and strange doctrine contrary to God's word, and both privately and openly to call upon and encourage other to the same?

Answer. I am ready, the Lord being my helper.

The Archbishop. Will you deny all ungodliness, and worldly lusts, and live soberly, righteously, and Godly in this world, that you may shew yourself in all things an example of good works unto other, that the adversary may be ashamed, having nothing to lay against you?

Answer. I will so do, the Lord being my helper.

The Archbishop. Will you maintain and set forward (as much as shall lie in you) quietness, peace, and love, among all men? And such as be unquiet, disobedient, and criminous within your diocese, correct and punish, according to such authority, as ye have by God's word, and as to you shall be committed, by the ordinance of this realm?

Answer. I will so do, by the help of God.

The Archbishop. Will you shew yourself gentle, and be merciful for Christ's sake, to poor and needy people, and to all strangers destitute of help?

Answer. I will so shew myself by God's grace.

The Archbishop. Almighty God our heavenly Father, who hath given you a good will to do all these things, grant also unto you strength and power, to perform the same, that he accomplishing in you the good work which he hath begun, ye may be found perfect, and irreprehensible at the latter day, through Jesu Christ our Lord. Amen.

Then shall be sung or said, Come Holy Ghost, *&c. as it is set out in the Order of Priests.*

That ended, the Archbishop shall say,

The Lord be with you.

Answer. And with thy spirit.

¶ Let us pray.

ALMIGHTY God and most merciful Father, which of thy infinite goodness, hast given to us thy only and most dear beloved Son Jesus Christ, to be our redeemer and author of everlasting life, who after that he had made perfect our redemption by his death, and was ascended into heaven, poured down his gifts abundantly upon men, making some Apostles, some Prophets, some Evangelists, some Pastors and Doctors, to the edifying and making perfect of his congregation: Grant, we beseech thee, to this thy servant such grace, that he may be evermore ready to spread abroad thy Gospel, and glad tidings of reconcilement to God, and to use the authority given unto him, not to destroy, but to save, not to hurt, but to help, so that he as a faithful and a wise servant, giving to thy family meat in due season, may at the last day be received into joy, through Jesu Christ our Lord, who with thee and the Holy Ghost liveth and reigneth one God, world without end. Amen.

Then the Archbishop and Bishops present shall lay their hands upon the head of the elect Bishop, the Archbishop saying.

TAKE the Holy Ghost, and remember that thou stir up the grace of God, which is in thee, by imposition of hands: for God hath not given us the spirit of fear, but of power, and love, and of soberness.

Then the Archbishop shall lay the Bible upon his neck, saying.

GIVE heed unto reading, exhortation and doctrine, think upon those things contained in this book, be diligent in them, that the increase coming thereby may be manifest unto all men. Take heed unto thyself, and unto teaching, and be diligent in doing them, for by doing this thou shalt save thyself and them that hear thee, through Jesus Christ our Lord.

Then shall the Archbishop put into his hand the pastoral staff, saying:

BE to the flock of Christ a shepherd, not a wolf, feed them, devour them not, hold up the weak, heal the sick, bind together the broken, bring again the outcasts, seek the lost: Be so merciful, that you be not too remiss, so minister discipline, that ye forget not mercy, that when the chief Shepherd shall come, ye may receive the immarcessible Crown of glory, through Jesus Christ our Lord.

¶ *Then the Archbishop shall proceed to the Communion, with whom the new consecrated Bishop shall also communicate. And after the last Collect, immediately afore the benediction, shall be said this prayer:*

MOST merciful Father, we beseech thee to send down upon this thy Servant thy heavenly blessing, and so endue him with thy Holy Spirit, that he preaching thy word, may not only be earnest to reprove, beseech, and rebuke with all patience and Doctrine, but also may be to such as believe an wholesome example in word, in conversation, in love, in faith, in chastity, and purity, that faithfully fulfilling his course, at the latter day he may receive the crown of righteousness, laid up by the Lord, the righteous Judge, who liveth and reigneth, one God with the Father and Holy Ghost, world without end. Amen.

www.ingramcontent.com/pod-product-compliance
Lightning Source LLC
Chambersburg PA
CBHW021802230426
43669CB00008B/607